Bill understands the cultural landscape [...]
paced, unpredictable, and ever-changing [...]
practical guidance and foundational principles in this book
are essential for building communities with greater impact
and effectiveness in today's world.

MARVIN CAMPBELL, US president of The Navigators

Typically, resources on leadership are about achieving better
performance, effectiveness, and outcomes. But this book is
refreshingly different: It focuses on what the leader must
become to wisely impact the cultures they serve in practical
and transformative ways. This is the kind of leader that
doesn't crash and burn.

Bill Mowry's writing is insightful yet easy to understand.
He brings clarity and practicality to the question of how to lead
from ordinary life assignments for extraordinary influence and
impact. His examples bring clarity combined with exercises
to maximize learning. Bill's writing style draws the reader
in—inviting the reader to walk the pathway that leads to a
relationally wise, emotionally intelligent, and spiritually astute
leader.

PATTI DAMIANI, Relational Wisdom ministry consultant (RW360)

This world needs leaders, men and women of courage and
character with learners' hearts. How can we grow as people—
as individuals and in our families, workplaces, and places of
worship—who influence with cultural wisdom and innovation?
This is the beauty and power of Bill's writing. He provides
practical and concrete tools that can be practiced in our

everyday lives. A much-needed resource in our world filled with polarization, silos, and independence.

LINDY BLACK, associate US director of The Navigators

Once again, Bill Mowry has given us an excellent book that is steeped in wisdom, refined by years of ministry experience, and inviting in tone. He builds a sturdy bridge from biblical principles to life practices as he guides leaders toward the competencies they need to respond to the rapidly changing challenges in our culture today. I highly recommend it!

DAN ESTES, distinguished professor of Old Testament at Cedarville University

In these changing, challenging times for church leaders comes a winsome book on gaining what we most need: wisdom. In *The Ways of The Leader*, Bill Mowry offers ministry leaders a resource on how to discern the wisest path forward through collegial learning, collaboration, contextual understanding, and innovative practices. This book is filled with anecdotes and quotes that will keep you engaged and reflecting. I look forward to using it with my team to gain the depth of insight we need to know how to reach our city. There are no silver bullets, no simple prescriptions for our times. We need to walk the way of wisdom and let God light our path. Thank you, Bill, for guiding us down that road in such a clear manner! A must-read for all leaders!

DAVE JANSEN, lead pastor for CenterPoint Church

This new book of Bill's is so practical, full of hope, and rich with examples. Biblical and relevant principles are supported with a plethora of tools and applications that can make the way of wisdom a reality for the everyday disciple as well as the leader. The entire book is very helpful, but I especially love the last chapter on the choices leaders face, so pertinent to our culture and time—it's a gem!

MARGARET FITZWATER, Navigators national leadership, executive director Train-Develop-Care

Immensely practical! This book offers tools and principles that leaders can immediately put into practice, no matter their ministry or experience.

CANDACE DOLPH, director of women's ministry at Linworth Baptist Church

The Ways of the Leader is so engagingly simple that it removes leadership from the realm of the elite and places it within reach of anyone pursuing the way of wisdom. What is the way of wisdom? Don't worry, Bill clarifies and makes that beautifully tangible also. In *The Ways of the Alongsider*, Bill puts disciplemaking back into the hands of the everyday Christ-follower. In *The Ways of the Leader*, he makes key principles of leadership equally accessible for us all.

AL ENGLER, senior VP of field ministries at The Navigators

Bill has delivered a wise and winsome road map for everyday leaders to follow with confidence and hope as we move toward greater innovation and impact in the face of accelerating change. I have known Bill for four decades. He is a thinking practitioner who models these principles. Every leader I know would benefit greatly from the journey Bill invites us on in this excellent book. Well done!

EVAN GRIFFIN, communication professor and Navigator representative at the University of Cincinnati

The Ways of the Leader is timely, powerful, and a must-read for leaders of all ages. Leaders everywhere are facing the need to navigate the fastballs of change that often come with cultural and generational challenges. Bill reminds us all that successful (fruitful) leaders are on a path of continual learning and use everyday life as a classroom to live and lead like Jesus. The application of this wisdom becomes the key to their success and is a distance marker of being a disciple of Jesus.

GINA HOLM, associate director of Nav Life, leadership coach for Train-Develop-Care and Navigators Church Ministries

Christian leaders today are stepping into the unknown—into an unexplored country that exhibits hopelessness in ways that compound the challenges of leadership. Bill Mowry has given these leaders a biblically grounded set of tools which will free them from the distractions and inertia of "what worked in the past." For those who are called to bring hope to hopeless situations, he illuminates essential tools of personal and cultural wisdom, learning, collaboration, and innovation to prepare them for God-glorifying, Christ-following leadership.

You won't find simplistic answers or formulas here. This book is a practical, strategic collection of tools to apply to your unique contexts. If you sense you are stepping into the unknown, wondering how to lead others in a Christ-centered exploration, this book is for you.

JOHN MESSER, regional executive of RCA's Synod of the Great Lakes

Bill has always excelled at being a skilled mentor and broad-range thinker around how leaders can grow in both character and vision. With its consistent bent toward lifelong learning and openness to exploration and its readiness to serve and strengthen others, *The Ways of the Leader* reflects his life's work, a remarkable combination of spiritual depth and intellectual curiosity. Bill's focus on journey over destination provides freedom to the reader, allowing application across a range of situations and leadership considerations. Truly wisdom and love are the guides through an ever-changing landscape.

JOSH ANTONUCCIO, professor of media arts and studies, Ohio University's Scripps College of Communication

The Ways of the Leader is an insightful look at the current need for new leaders in a time of rapid sociocultural change. This isn't the typical book on leadership that tells you how to become a megastar. Bill describes leadership as the application of the principles of godly wisdom. This isn't a how-to book but a tool kit that will assist you to be the leader that God has designed you to be where he has placed you.

J. RUPERT MORGAN, PhD, resident missiologist at ABWE International

This book is the cure for "quick fix" formulas! And it couldn't be any timelier. Prescriptions won't work in the polarizing time we are in. A seasoned leader like Bill Mowry knows there is only one way through the chaos of our time. It's not a solution from an expert in another context. You will need to grow the deeper ways of wisdom that can help you navigate the uncharted terrain of your particular place and time. I highly recommend you get your people together and take a very deep dive into *The Ways of the Leader*.

PAUL SPARKS, coauthor of the award-winning book *The New Parish: How Neighborhood Churches Are Transforming Mission, Discipleship and Community*

BILL MOWRY

The Ways of the Leader

*Four Practices to Bring People Together
and Break New Ground*

A NavPress resource published in alliance
with Tyndale House Publishers

NavPress.com

The Ways of the Leader: Four Practices to Bring People Together and Break New Ground

Copyright © 2023 by Bill Mowry. All rights reserved.

A NavPress resource published in alliance with Tyndale House Publishers

NavPress and the NavPress logo are registered trademarks of NavPress, The Navigators, Colorado Springs, CO. *Tyndale* is a registered trademark of Tyndale House Ministries. Absence of ® in connection with marks of NavPress or other parties does not indicate an absence of registration of those marks.

The Team:
David Zimmerman, Publisher; Deborah Sáenz Gonzalez, Acquisitions Editor; Jennifer Lonas, Copyeditor; Olivia Eldredge, Operations Manager; Libby Dykstra, Designer

Cover design by Libby Dykstra.

Unless otherwise noted, interior icons are the property of their respective copyright holders from The Noun Project, and all rights are reserved. Team © birdpeople; magnifying glass © Pedro Santos; lightbulb © Farra Nugraha; path by Laura Cruise © Tyndale House Ministries.

Author photograph copyright © 2022 by Bill Mowry. All rights reserved.

Visit alongsider.com for archives of the author's prior writing, teaching, and training, some of which informs, is paraphrased or quoted in, and is drawn from in this work.

Some of the anecdotal illustrations in this book are true to life and are included with the permission of the persons involved. All other illustrations are composites of real situations, and any resemblance to people living or dead is purely coincidental.

For information about special discounts for bulk purchases, please contact Tyndale House Publishers at csresponse@tyndale.com, or call 1-855-277-9400.

ISBN 978-1-64158-669-6

Printed in the United States of America

29 28 27 26 25 24 23
7   6   5   4   3   2   1

To Peggy, my friend, my partner, my love, my wife. In our nearly five decades together, God has used you to help me be a better disciple, leader, and author. Thank you!

Contents

The Challenge Before Us

Leading in Uncharted Territory

Things fall apart; the centre cannot hold;
Mere anarchy is loosed upon the world,
The blood-dimmed tide is loosed, and everywhere
The ceremony of innocence is drowned.

W. B. YEATS, "THE SECOND COMING"

IT'S TIME FOR TENNIS PRACTICE. You assume the ready stance and anxiously wait for the machine to throw the first ball. Here it comes! You hit it squarely, but before you can recover your stance, another ball is coming at you. Then another . . . and another. The balls are coming so fast, you have no time to recover.

Welcome to leadership in the twenty-first century.

Leading today is like tennis practice when the ball machine is throwing fastballs. The fastballs of change keep coming at us! We barely have time to recover from the last swing before a new ball is headed our way.

The recent COVID pandemic was one of these fastballs of change. The pandemic accelerated several significant cultural changes: We've endured political transitions and a redefining of employment, and many of us now have a heightened awareness of racism. Lockdowns and quarantines challenged how we "do church." The centers of our culture, our churches, and our lives are barely holding.

Pastor and consultant Tod Bolsinger notes that we're in uncharted territory. "The world in front of you is nothing like the world behind you," he writes.[1] "Today's leaders are facing complex challenges that have no clear-cut solutions. . . . They can't be solved through a conference, a video series or a program. . . . We have to learn to lead all over again."[2]

We not only must lead differently, but we also need different kinds of leaders—heroic leaders who will know how to bring people together to break new ground.

Heroes are the people we admire for their life examples or good deeds. They're the people we put on a pedestal, the people we name our children after, the people we aspire to be like. Today, in our church and social culture, we're championing a certain type of hero—the highly trained professional leader. I'm writing to restore the hero of the everyday leader.

Why do we need these new heroes? The traditional hero of the megachurch pastor, the business executive, or the ministry leader is facing hard times. Almost daily, we hear how these traditional leaders—both inside and outside the church—fall through indiscretion or moral failure. We've created expectations about our leaders that no one person can satisfy.

We need new heroes because the traditional solitary leader's expertise is no longer adequate for the rapid changes in our culture. What works in one setting does not automatically transfer to another. Local challenges demand something more than an imported, one-size-fits-all approach.

We need everyday leaders who bring people together to break new ground—crafting *local* solutions for *local* challenges. They don't outsource problems to distant experts who think and plan for them. Instead, they practice four biblical ways that create local strategies for local challenges.

Who are these everyday leaders? They can lack impressive titles, the coveted corner offices, or the resource of multiple staff. They're small- or mid-size church pastors, ministry leaders, community activists, and workplace influencers. These men and women often face the fastballs of change by themselves or with a limited staff or with volunteers. These everyday leaders are everywhere, serving in small and unnoticed places.

Everyday leaders are marked by three simple qualities. First, they have a love for the local expressed in an urgency to help neighborhoods, workplaces, or churches succeed and flourish. You could say they "own" the local; they're emotionally invested in the people and places closest to them.

Second, everyday leaders display Jesus in their lives. They value character over competency. Who they are is more important than what they can do.

Finally, in small and large ways, everyday leaders provide direction. They want to influence their workplaces, make their neighborhoods better, or encourage their churches to be more missional. They desire local strategies for local challenges.

Everyday leaders realize that solutions designed by distant experts may not be relevant in local settings. They need new ways to wisely think, serve, and lead. What new ways are needed to bring people together to break new ground?

Welcome to *The Ways of the Leader*. Be alert! This book will not provide you with solutions or answers, but it will give you tools you can use to wisely develop your own strategies and solutions for local challenges.

Most of this book is targeted for church and ministry leaders. This is the arena in which I've lived and ministered for the past forty years. However, the principles and practices I will be sharing can be used by any leader in any setting. Whether you're leading in business, school, church ministry, or neighborhood, you can profit from this book.

No matter who you are, you're on the tennis court of life and ministry facing three fastballs of change. How you handle these balls will determine your effectiveness as a leader.

Ball No. 1: We Live in the Fast Lane

Our culture is addicted to speed. We want faster smartphones, laptops, and customer service. I find myself impatiently tapping my foot if I have to wait in line or on a phone call longer than a few minutes. Don't people know I'm in a hurry?

Author Thomas Friedman writes that the pace of change in our culture is challenging our ability to adapt. Citing a conversation with Eric Teller, the CEO of X, Google's research lab, Friedman summarizes: "Change is now accelerating so fast that it has risen above the average rate at which most people can absorb all these changes. Many of us cannot keep pace anymore."[3]

Friedman and Teller are discussing technological change in society. However, we feel this change at a personal level in our everyday lives and ministries. Change is outstripping our ability to keep pace. The tennis balls keep coming at us! Our speed addiction shows up when words like *linger*, *saunter*, *stroll*, and *amble* have all but disappeared from our vocabularies, along with casual synonyms like *stray, range, roam, ramble,* and *wander.*[4] There's an unspoken expectation, writes Carl Honoré, for people to "think faster, work faster, talk faster, read faster, write faster, eat faster, and move faster."[5] I feel tired already!

Life in the fast lane values screen time over think time. According to author Nicholas Carr, "It's often assumed that the time we devote to the Net [and other social media] comes out of the time we would otherwise spend watching TV. But statistics suggest otherwise. Most studies of media activity indicate that as Net use has gone up, television viewing has either held steady or increased."[6]

One everyday leader told me about creating a device-free zone in his home. "When I wake up," he said, "I immediately pick up my phone or iPad to check for messages. When a screen is present, I look at it. I can only slow down to think when these devices are absent."

Our busy schedules have placed us in a position where "we devote ever less time to the calmer, more attentive modes of thinking that have always given richness to our intellectual lives and our culture."[7] The richness that comes from slowing down aids the creative process.

Carl Honoré notes, "Research has shown that people think more creatively when they are calm, unhurried and free from stress, and that time pressure leads to tunnel vision."[8] Speed and busyness do not set the stage for creativity.

Staying in the fast lane creates superficial thinking; we end up "skim[ming] the surface, and fail[ing] to make real connections with the world or other people."[9] This failure to make connections prevents us from responding in new and fresh ways to the challenges around us. For everyday leaders, moving out of the fast lane means countering the fastball of speed.

Ball No. 2: We Live with Black Swans

For hundreds of years, people assumed that all swans were white. No one thought that a black swan could exist because they had seen only white swans. Then black swans were discovered in Australia, and everyone's conceptions of the swan family were upended. The worlds of swan lovers everywhere were shattered! Welcome to life among black swans.

In his book *The Black Swan*, Nassim Taleb describes a black swan as a positive or negative event that is deemed improbable and yet causes massive consequences. Black swan events are unpredictable, but once they occur, they upset our personal or cultural realities.[10]

The 9/11 attacks on the World Trade Center and Pentagon were black swan events. No one predicted that a small group of al-Qaeda sympathizers would terrorize the Western world using passenger jets as weapons. Donald Trump's election was a black swan event. Few predicted that he would be elected president, and his election turned the political world upside down. COVID-19 was another black swan event. While many scientists foresaw the possibility of a worldwide pandemic, no one predicted the virus's timing and subsequent impact on economies, politics, or education.

Why are black swan events impactful? Taleb argues that we make assumptions and predictions about the future based on the belief that our current reality will continue to be our future reality. What is true now gives us the comfort to predict the future. Seldom do we take into account the unexpected or the unpredictable.

As leaders, how do we respond to black swan events? What

skills do we need to live and minister in the middle of these events? If they're unpredictable, then the easy answers we desire will not magically appear. There are no easy answers when life is unpredictable and the future may not be like the present. Our familiar ways of doing things will have to be discarded as we deal with black swan events on multiple levels.

Ball No. 3: We Live in a Culturally Diverse Nation

What does ministry look like in a diverse culture? Each immigrant and refugee family comes to America with culturally ingrained values regarding societal norms, education, religion, finances, and family life. How can everyday leaders understand and adapt to the variety of cultural elements within their cities, neighborhoods, businesses, and churches?

The old ministry models formed in a homogeneous culture are inadequate for today's challenges. Our culture is changing, and this change is reflected in the US Census Bureau's redistricting data on racial and ethnic groups in the 2020 national census.[11] What do the results tell us about the diversity of our nation?

- "Nearly four of 10 Americans identify with a race or ethnic group other than white."
- "Racial and ethnic minorities accounted for all of the nation's population growth."
- The Hispanic population has now outpaced the African American population (18.5% and 12.5% of the total population, respectively).
- "More than half of the nation's population under age 16 identified as a racial or ethnic minority."

These statistics reveal that our nation is becoming more racially diverse from the bottom up by generation. In a few short decades, white culture will no longer be dominant in the US. The younger generation is not only more diverse but also thinks about diversity in different ways than the established older generation.

How do we lead in a nation that is rapidly becoming more diverse demographically? How do we respond with sensitivity and respect for cultures that are different from ours? What changes will this increased diversity bring to ministry, business, and church life? Local everyday leaders must learn to think, plan, and lead differently in an increasingly diverse culture.

We Need New Ways to Counter
the Fastballs of Change

Two challenges are becoming obvious. The first is that standard solutions are losing their ability to meet these fastballs of change. Gone are the days when a ministry or business "franchise" could be imported from one successful church, business, or ministry to another. A one-size-fits-all approach can no longer guarantee the same results in Portland, Cleveland, or Atlanta.

The second challenge is that the expertise of traditional solitary leaders is no longer adequate for the rapid changes in our culture. Few leaders are equipped to meet the challenges of social media, changing economic realities, and an increasingly diverse culture. These fastballs stretch and at times nullify the effectiveness of the solitary leader.

The solution I propose doesn't require expensive budgets, high-priced consultants, or elaborate programs. Nor does it call for more personnel, a different strategic plan, or more buildings. The solution is pretty simple: Everyday leaders must practice God's way of wisdom, employing four wisdom-generating practices. Wisdom is the everyday leader's partner in our journey of life and ministry.

This wisdom and the four wisdom-generating practices are necessary to create local strategies for local challenges. With the guidance of the Holy Spirit and these four practices, you can bring people together to break new ground.

Practice #1. The way of learning. Everyday leaders are learners who know how to extract wisdom from the rhythms and routines of life. Life and ministry are God's classroom to teach and instruct us. We don't need simply another leadership seminar; we need to practice the way of lifelong learning.

Practice #2. The way of collaboration. Everyday leaders capture the power of people working collaboratively and wisely with others to develop new strategies for local challenges. Collaboration draws upon the wisdom in the group.

Practice #3. The way of cultural wisdom. Everyday leaders need cultural wisdom to understand and connect with the people they lead and minister to in specific contexts. To do this, they must become culture detectives, collecting clues about these contexts in order to lead more wisely and effectively.

Practice #4. The way of innovation. Everyday leaders create innovative strategies to meet local challenges. They redeem their birthrights as creators and employ their God-given imaginations in wise and innovative ways.

There's a natural flow to these four practices. When leaders become **lifelong learners**, they know how to extract wisdom from everyday life that gives insight to life and ministry challenges. This learning not only grows godly wisdom in their personal and leadership lives but also sparks the fire of learning in those around them.

Learning is the cornerstone of **collaboration**. Collaboration starts with a recognition that one person does not have all the answers but must draw upon the wisdom of the community around him or her to develop new strategies and solutions. When learning is modeled and encouraged, a natural reservoir of wisdom opens up in a local church, workplace, or neighborhood.

All leadership takes place in a context, a culture of people. If we're bringing people together to break new ground, then we must first understand the current "ground," or culture. **Cultural wisdom** is a natural outgrowth of individual and collective learning about the context in which we live, work, or minister.

For **innovation** to be effective, it must make sense for that particular culture and the people in it. Cultural wisdom shapes and provides a context for innovation to happen. As the agrarian philosopher and novelist Wendell Berry writes, "You have to fit the farming to the land."[12] If a farmer doesn't understand the land, then the crops will fail. In the same way, if our great, innovative ideas are irrelevant to our context, then those innovations are useless.

What happens when these four ways are practiced? The Holy Spirit allows us to grow in wisdom—the ability to choose the good and the right.

I cannot overemphasize that this is a flow and not a mechanistic, step-by-step process. Some of the practices may be more relevant than others to your challenges. Some "steps" may demand less time. Leaders will need wisdom to decide what is good and right for their local settings.

It's my prayer and hope that these four ways of leading will become part of your life and ministry.

How to Use This Book

I recommend using one of the following approaches as you engage with the content in this book.

1. Read the book in its entirety to gain an overview of the four ways or practices.

2. Use this resource like a cookbook, reading and applying one practice at a time. Just as you wouldn't make all the recipes in a cookbook at the same time, so you won't immediately apply all four ways of leading.

3. Treat this book as a series of progressive exercises where you take a group of people sequentially through the four practices. This process will yield the best results when you identify a specific challenge or problem rather than simply reading the material together.

4. View it as a training manual for ministry or leadership development. For example, I suggest that every leader in a church or ministry immediately apply the practice of life-long learning.

5. Use this book as a blueprint for personal development. At the end of the book are practice assignments to help you apply the ways of learning. You can pick and choose one or more of these assignments to learn how to use the practice(s) described.

However you engage with this book, I hope that it will enable you to lead in ways that bring people together to break new ground. I invite you to start this journey by meeting our journey's partner—Lady Wisdom.

Wisdom Is the Ultimate Way

Wisdom is the everyday leader's partner in our journey of life and ministry.

Throughout the Bible, we are constantly challenged
to learn God's wisdom, to live God's wisdom, and
to love God's wisdom.

DANIEL ESTES, *THE MESSAGE OF WISDOM*

I WAS A SLIGHTLY ARROGANT and ambitious leader when I joined the Navigators staff at the age of twenty-five. I had a history of authority issues coupled with a know-it-all attitude. I didn't need a supervisor who would tell me what to do or lecture me on life and ministry. The Lord took my immaturity into consideration and assigned the right boss for me.

John Ed Robertson was my first Navigators supervisor. He was a former naval officer with a degree in nuclear engineering—a subject that immediately made him smarter than me. John Ed had a bit of an absent-minded-professor look about him, making him likable and approachable. What sealed our relationship was the discovery that we were both Bob Dylan fans.

John Ed never pretended to have all the answers. In fact, he often talked more about his failures than his victories. I observed that he was on a life and ministry learning curve—always experimenting, always learning, always growing. He seldom passed on to others ministry formulas or packaged answers; he encouraged people to grow in wisdom.

As a new staff member, I was looking for solutions and models to be successful. I often asked questions like "What's the best way to do this?" "What do I do next?" "What are others doing that I can do?" In other words, "What's the best program that will bring ministry success?"

Instead of being the wise sage giving solutions, John Ed modeled two practices that helped move me from ministry formulas to wise living and gave me a pattern to help others live wisely. First, he asked questions and told stories. John Ed reined in a boss's natural inclination to tell and asked instead. His example taught me to ask questions, reflect on life's events, and learn. He also did one more thing. Within the context of our Navigators vision, John Ed supported my innovative approaches and helped me learn from my mistakes and successes. He never said, "This is what Navigators are supposed to do" or "You can't do that in The Navigators." His trust in the Lord, and in me, gave me the freedom to learn, and from this freedom I grew in wisdom.

It was years before I fully appreciated John Ed's wise approach. At the time I wanted success, but he gave wisdom. His way of leading prepared me for life, not for the moment. This is what wisdom does; it enables us to think and adapt, not plug and play.

Meet Our Partner

Before we begin our walk through the four practices we must first meet our life and leadership partner. You will enjoy this companion. She is peaceable, gentle, open to reason, and full of mercy and good fruits. Not only that but she's impartial and sincere. Without her partnership you will not be able to bring people together to break new ground. Her name is Wisdom, and she has been my unseen ministry partner for more than forty years.

Wisdom in the Bible is personified as a woman (Proverbs 1:20; 8:1; 9:1). Scholar Bruce Waltke describes her as "a unique woman who wears the mantle of a prophet, carries the scrolls of wise men, and wears a goddess-like diadem."[1] Lady Wisdom, "in all her various guises, . . . personifies Solomon's inspired wisdom."[2]

Unlike the other woman in Proverbs, the seductress who hides in dark corners luring men to her bed (7:6-18), Lady Wisdom stands in the open places, at the crossroads, by the city gates (8:1-3). Wisdom makes herself known where people meet and talk. "There's nothing furtive, nothing underhand, about Wisdom," writes theologian David Atkinson.[3]

Lady Wisdom is the "epitome of all that is good and right and lovely."[4] In Proverbs 9:1-6, she goes to great effort and expense to prepare a meal for her guests, intentionally setting a beautiful table. Why all this care? She's inviting us to "leave [our] simple ways and . . . live; walk in the way of insight" (verse 6). Lady Wisdom is inviting us to the sumptuous life of wisdom, to a way of living.

Atkinson writes that "this personification of Wisdom is not a (mere) literary device; it reflects the essential nature of biblical wisdom. Wisdom is embodied. Wisdom is for living."[5] Pastor and theologian Eugene Peterson explained that when we personalize Wisdom as a woman, "we find ourselves listening to a person rather than following a handbook of instructions."[6] Wisdom is not found in the accumulation of information but in the flesh-and-blood experiences and insight of people walking with God.

For decades, Lady Wisdom has figuratively stood by me giving insight, understanding, and discernment in ministry crises, marital challenges, and life-and-death moments. I could not have lived life without her.

Everyday leaders need Lady Wisdom's partnership to hit the fastballs of change they encounter. Unfortunately, wisdom seldom comes up as a topic of conversation when I talk with leaders. You would think that the acquisition and practice of wisdom would be the number one task for leaders today. I think we too easily make turnkey programs or curricula our partners.

Turnkey programs are designed by what I call "learning mercenaries"—the professional seminar leader or bestselling author who has done the learning work for us. Sometimes it's more convenient to have someone tell us the answers than teach us how to discover the answers ourselves. When we outsource wisdom, we unknowingly choose expediency over thinking for ourselves with the mind of Christ. Employing a learning mercenary is the easy way; our Lord invites us to the hard way, the way of wisdom.

Wisdom is the hard way, but it's a way available to everyone—every leader who struggles with rapid change, unexpected crises, or cultural challenges. Lady Wisdom invites us to her table, and all we have to do is accept her invitation. This is a lifeline for leaders with limited resources. God in his compassion has provided a resource available to anyone anywhere.

Lady Wisdom is found in the commands of the Bible, she guides us through biblical principles, and she walks with us through life's experiences. When everyday leaders walk with Lady Wisdom, they walk in a distinctive way.

What is this wise way? What characterizes godly wisdom? Let's plunge into some answers for these questions.

Lady Wisdom Invites Us to a Way of Life

My son Jason is a professional illustrator. He illustrates high-end books, exhibits in galleries around the world, and is featured in top-tier illustration magazines. There's a way about his work that distinguishes him from other artists. This "way" is a personalized style that sends a message: "I'm created by Jason Mowry."

We all have a way of doing things. A "way" describes a style, a personality that gives definition to someone or something. This way makes us stand out in a crowd. When we talk about the way of wisdom, we're describing a lifestyle, a way of living. Being wise is how everyday leaders live.

References to the concept of a "way" show up repeatedly in the biblical record. In Psalm 128:1, we discover that the blessed person is the one "who walks in [God's] ways" (ESV). This way of life also shows up in the Wisdom Literature of the Old Testament. Daniel Estes, an Old Testament scholar, notes that "the most prominent image in the book of Proverbs is represented by the term *derek*, which in its over seventy uses in Proverbs speaks of the path, way or journey of life."[7] In the New Testament, we discover that early Christianity was called "the Way" (Acts 9:2, 22:4, 24:14).

Our life and journey with God speaks of a way, a path of wisdom, a lifestyle to be lived.

What marks a wise lifestyle? Here's a sampling of Scripture passages on the importance of wisdom:

If only they were wise and would understand this and discern what their end will be! (Deuteronomy 32:29)

[Make] your ear attentive to wisdom and [incline] your heart to understanding. (Proverbs 2:2, ESV)

A man will be commended according to his wisdom. (Proverbs 12:8, NKJV)

Therefore everyone who hears these words of mine and puts them into practice is like a wise man. (Matthew 7:24)

I want you to be wise about what is good, and innocent about what is evil. (Romans 16:19)

Admonish one another with all wisdom. (Colossians 3:16)

If any of you lacks wisdom, you should ask God, who gives generously to all. (James 1:5)

The wisdom from above is first pure, then peaceable, gentle, open to reason. (James 3:17, ESV)

Coming up with a tidy definition for *wisdom* is like trying to nail Jell-O to a wall. It's much easier to give a credible description of the concept. Here is my working description: *Wisdom skillfully chooses what is good and right.* When I talk about the *way* of wisdom, I'm referring to *a lifestyle where one skillfully chooses the good and the right.* Let's unpack this description.

Thinking of wisdom as a **skill** shouldn't surprise us. One of the Hebrew words for *wisdom* (*ḥokmâ*) means "being 'skillful' in a variety of practical and artistic [practices]."[8] "When it is used in an ethical sense," writes Daniel Estes, "it has the nuance of skill in living . . . specifically to skill in living according to the Lord's moral order."[9]

Skill describes an ability to do something well. The crew that remodeled my bathroom had skills in laying tile, electricity, and plumbing. Through experience and knowledge, they had accumulated wisdom that allowed them to skillfully complete the jobs.

When faced with a new challenge, they drew upon their skills—their wisdom—to do what was good and right for the job at hand.

Wisdom is always a **choice**. In Proverbs I'm presented with the choice between the wise and the foolish (1:32-33). Jesus challenges us to make a choice between the wide gate and the narrow gate (Matthew 7:13-14). With the Spirit's guidance, I choose the good and the right.

When we speak of what's **good**, we speak of God's essential character. He is "abundant in goodness and truth" (Exodus 34:6, KJV). Theologian J. I. Packer writes that "this is the quality of generosity . . . a disposition to give to others in a way which has no mercenary motive and is not limited by what the recipients deserve."[10] Being good means giving life and nourishment to others, the essence of blessing.

When we think about what's **right**, we consider what is appropriate or the right thing to do. The Scriptures take this a step further in describing what is right as the moral outcome of wisdom. Doing the right thing is choosing to walk in a way that conforms to God's righteous standard, doing what is just and fair (Proverbs 1:3, 2:20). Packer writes that "the biblical judge is expected to love justice and fair play and to loathe all ill-treatment of man by his fellow-man. . . . A judge wholly [identifies] with what is good and right."[11]

"What is right (*ṣedeq*)," says Daniel Estes, "refers to what conforms to the Lord's righteous standard, what is just (*mišpāṭ*) indicates the proper way to behave, and what is fair (*mēšārîm*) speaks of honesty and fairness."[12] Wisdom is the ability to choose what is right, just, and fair, a way that aligns with God's moral character.

When I speak of lifestyle, I speak of a way of living. Wisdom is not a moral code to follow (though there are biblical commands);

it points to a way of living—a pattern of values, beliefs, and actions—where I choose what is good and right. Wisdom is something more than making Yoda-like pronouncements; wisdom marks how we live.

Estes speaks to the importance of a wise lifestyle, noting that "wisdom . . . is much more than acquiring a lot of knowledge and instruction, but rather it is the ability to assess situations wisely, to make good decisions and to act responsibly."[13] In other words, wisdom is a life to live, not information to master; a mindset, not a set of rules or fixed formulas. Wisdom is skillfully choosing what is good and right.

How do we gain this wisdom? By following Lady Wisdom's three paths.

Lady Wisdom's Three Paths

Lady Wisdom has three paths for the everyday leader: the fixed path, the principled path, and the experiential path. Woven together with the Holy Spirit's assistance, these paths give a robust, rich, and flavorful picture of a wise life. Everyday leaders need to be able to recognize which of these paths is necessary to deal with everyday challenges.

Fixed → Obey the commands
Principled → Practice applicatory thinking
Experiential → Learn from life: observe, reflect, interpret

Some wisdom is **fixed**—prescribed and defined—in commands and precepts. The Lord established the fixed nature of his wisdom in the Ten Commandments (Exodus 20:1-17) and the subsequent instructions in the Pentateuch. Israel swore to keep his commandments, making it a life-or-death decision (Deuteronomy 30:11-20). Keeping his commandments would show the nations how wise they were and how wise their God was (4:5-8). We gain wisdom about life and death from the fixed nature of God's commands.

Fixed wisdom tells us that adultery is never a good thing (Exodus 20:14), theft is not a lifestyle to practice (Ephesians 4:28), and loving others is not optional (John 13:34-35). There's a fixed nature to these commands with little wiggle room for declining obedience.

However, there's a limit to fixed-command thinking. Sometimes the explicit command may not address a morally ambiguous situation. We find few fixed commands to counter the fastballs we swing at every day. Where do we find wisdom outside these fixed commands?

Lady Wisdom's second path gives insight into meeting today's fastballs of change. This path is a **principled** path—applying biblical principles to the challenges that fixed commands do not address.

Principles are guiding truths, assumptions, or adaptive commands. Estes describes the principled nature of Proverbs as being characterized by "guidelines rather than fixed formulas."[14] Biblical principles are guidelines. Let me illustrate by demonstrating how Proverbs addresses evangelism in a principled way. Proverbs is not known as a book that speaks specifically about evangelism. However, we can glean some wonderful principles of wisdom from Proverbs 27:14 (ESV):

Whoever blesses his neighbor with a loud voice,
     rising early in the morning,
     will be counted as cursing.

This proverb teaches us how to have good relations with our neighbors. We can have a great message (a blessing) for a neighbor, but when it's shared at an inappropriate time ("early in the morning") and in an inappropriate way ("a loud voice"), it will be "counted as cursing." Good neighbors are sensitive about the timing and appropriateness of conversations.

How does this principle apply to evangelism? Wisdom tells us that conversing with others about the gospel must be done at appropriate times and in appropriate ways. We've all experienced indifference and even hostility when starting a spiritual conversation at the wrong time and in the wrong way. Evangelism is thwarted because we're not wise in our communication.

Does this proverb govern all evangelism? No. In fact, the passage is not about evangelism at all; it's about neighboring. However, the principles of good neighboring give us insight into how and when to share the good news with others. Wisdom is here found in the principles, not in the explicit command.

Carolyn Nystrom and J. I. Packer call this practice "the art of applicatory thinking." I love this phrase. Applicatory thinking thoughtfully identifies biblical principles that will lead to the greatest good and the least evil.[15] Applicatory thinking gives us insight, understanding, and discernment to respond in biblical ways to life and ministry issues—ways that are not met by fixed commands. How do we gain the ability to practice the art of applicatory thinking?

I was enjoying a casual conversation with Pastor Dwayne about what made his fifty-plus years of marriage and ministry so rich. One of his lessons surprised me: "When my wife and I got married, we decided to read through the Bible in our first year of marriage. We so enjoyed this exercise that we've done it every year since then."

My mind quickly added up the years of his marriage and concluded that Dwayne had read through the Bible more than fifty times! It's no wonder that when you poked him, the Bible came out. His whole life was filtered through the Scriptures. He's one of the most knowledgeable men of the Bible I know, and he's also prized for his wisdom. Dwayne's life has been soaked in the language of Scripture, which has enabled him to think as Jesus thought.

Applicatory thinking is drawn from a mind soaked in the Bible. We hear the wisdom of God in our heads because the Scriptures have become our first language of thinking. This type of thinking doesn't shoehorn truth, making it fit the same way in every setting. Principled thinking assists us in making good decisions in those areas without explicit instruction.

Wisdom leads to insight or understanding that may not be a repeatable "law." This wisdom can be local and personal; what's wise in one cultural setting may not transfer to another.

There's one more path that Lady Wisdom walks—a path everyone walks on: the **experiential** path.

One of my first jobs after college was working on a construction crew. To say that I was inexperienced is an understatement! The foreman, Gene, took a huge risk in hiring me.

Gene was a gruff, no-nonsense man with a big heart who treated me like a son. He taught me how to work and think in principled ways. Some of the principles came from the Bible, but most came from life experience.

When I faced a work challenge I couldn't solve, he would say, "Mowry, it can't think. Don't let it outfox you!" To teach me efficiency and teamwork, he would yell from a second-floor scaffolding, "Mowry, anticipate my next move! Anticipate!"

To protect my inexperience (and his credibility), he told me, "Mowry, when the man [homeowner] is watching you and you don't know how to do something, walk away and do something else. Never let the man know that you don't know what you're doing!"

Gene developed these insights from experience; he walked the path of experiential wisdom. Through experience and trial and error, he learned how to problem-solve, how to work efficiently, and how to relate to homeowners in credible ways.

Experiential wisdom is not found in my office or by sitting in a classroom. It's "truth that is intended to be learned and lived out in the world," writes Estes.[16] That's why Lady Wisdom calls out from the city gates: Her voice is found in the everyday experience of life's routines.

The book of Proverbs is full of experiential wisdom. Here are some examples:

Go to the ant, you sluggard;
consider its ways and be wise! (6:6)

With their mouths the godless destroy their neighbors. (11:9)

An excellent wife is the crown of her husband. (12:4, ESV)

Good sense wins favor. (13:15, ESV)

All hard work brings a profit,
but mere talk leads only to poverty. (14:23)

We can learn how to work by watching ants, discover that our conversations can destroy our neighbors, and experience the value of a wonderful spouse. We don't need fixed wisdom or biblical principles to come to these conclusions.

Experiential wisdom is gained by observing, experiencing, and then reflecting. We stop and think about what happened, what we learned, what we would keep doing or stop doing. This reflection, though, always has a filter, a grid through which we interpret our conclusions. That grid is "the mind of Christ" (1 Corinthians 2:16).

This mind is not governed by the flesh (Ephesians 2:3) or our old manner of life (4:17). It has been renewed, "created after the likeness of God in true righteousness and holiness" (4:23-24, ESV). This mind must be renewed and shaped by God's vantage point (Romans 12:2). Thinking like Jesus is an ongoing process that happens when we soak our minds and lives in the Scriptures.

We can form erroneous conclusions from life. We could conclude that "good guys finish last." We could deduce that "the grass is always greener on the other side." We could make "those with the most toys win" the bottom line of our lives. The writer of Ecclesiastes understood that forming conclusions only from observation and experience is like "chasing after the wind" (2:11). How do we elevate over these erroneous conclusions?

In her book *Walking on Water*, the late Madeleine L'Engle offered a helpful insight on trusting just our points of view: "In an interview in a well-known Christian magazine, I explained earnestly that we are limited by our points of view; 'I have a point of view,' I told the interviewer. 'You have a point of view. But *God* has *view*.'"[17] When we climb the high peak of God's point of view by saturating our minds with Scripture, we have the vantage point to interpret our conclusions from what we observe and experience.

Everyday leaders must be lifelong learners of the Bible, regularly practicing applicatory thinking (Psalm 1:1-3; 2 Timothy 2:15). When we soak in God's Word, the Bible becomes the prism through which all of life is filtered. The Bible equips us to think as Jesus thought. When everyday leaders are immersed in and filled with the life of the Scriptures (Colossians 3:16), they are guided by the Holy Spirit (Ephesians 5:18).

Theologian R. C. Lucas comments on the similarities of being filled with the Spirit and being filled with the Word in this way: "In Paul's teaching there is never any question of Word and Spirit being separately experienced. The coming of the Word of God in the gospel is the coming of the Spirit, and the coming of the Spirit is the coming of the living and abiding Word of God. Therefore, to enjoy the fullness of the Spirit, a Christian must necessarily be filled with the word of Christ."[18] When our minds and hearts are shaped by the Scriptures, we enable the Holy Spirit to lead and transform.

Lady Wisdom wonderfully blends together the fixed path, the principled path, and the experiential path through the ministry of the Holy Spirit. The Spirit is the one who ultimately gives insight and understanding, the ability to spot and choose God's ways. Life is a prayerful exercise of asking God to produce wisdom in our lives as we daily travel these three paths.

A Final Reflection: A Doctor of the Way

Dr. Bill is one of my current life mentors. He's an experienced physician working at a major research university. Bill is also a committed Christ-follower.

I call Bill a walking file cabinet of medical knowledge; his command of current medical research is amazing. At the same time, he has soaked his life in the Scriptures. At one of our breakfast meetings, he described spending an entire Sunday afternoon in the book of Philippians. He wasn't preparing a message; he just loved reading the Bible.

Bill's field of study is the relationship between stress and aging. We've enjoyed multiple breakfasts talking about how to deal with stress and how to replenish our lives. Bill pictures medicine as more of an art than a science. He wisely weaves together medical research with biblical principles.

There's a way about Bill that draws me to him, and that way is his wisdom. He has insight and discernment in life and medicine, places where there are few fixed rules. He artfully blends together the Bible with medical research and the experiential wisdom gained from years of treating patients. The Holy Spirit weaves all these paths into the way of wisdom.

Everyday leaders today face a barrage of new challenges. Some of the challenges can be met with clear biblical and moral imperatives. However, many challenges and the solutions we design for them have neither a biblical precedent nor a fixed moral command. We need the wisdom gained from Lady Wisdom's three paths to help us skillfully choose what is good and right. Like my friend Bill, we realize that life and leadership are more art than science. Wisdom is the cornerstone that enables us to bring people together to break new ground.

The Way of Learning

Everyday leaders are learners who extract wisdom from the rhythms and routines of life.

Learning is not only a lifelong task but also a lifelong summons to renewal of the soul.

JOAN CHITTISTER, *THE GIFT OF YEARS*

MY FIRST NAVIGATORS STAFF MEETING was a surprise. The surprise wasn't the agenda, the new faces, or the A-frame-cabin meeting place. It was the coffee-break conversations.

At the break, everyone began talking about the books they were reading. One staff member was attending seminary and discussed his latest book assignments; another described how he and his wife read each night before bed; and my supervisor, John Ed, always had a book in his briefcase. It seemed that I was the only one who wasn't a reader.

I discovered that this was more than an Oprah's Book Club session. These men and women read to learn. No one assigned these books; there wasn't a prescribed booklist. These leaders simply loved learning, and their love was infectious.

I found myself in a silent corner of the room having little to share. My learning experience was limited to a few well-read books and a meager Bible-study approach.

Our meetings and decisions were shaped by the staff's reading discoveries. We debated new ideas gleaned from reading, discussed how the Bible either affirmed or challenged these ideas, and talked together about questions raised. Learning happened through the intersection of the Scriptures, books, and life experiences. Reading books did not replace the Bible but drove people back to the Bible in fresh ways.

My coworkers' learning zeal grabbed my attention. Their examples taught me how to think about ministry, how to understand culture, and how to apply an author's insights to my setting. Oh, and one other thing happened: I soaked in the joy of learning. I learned how to be a learner, and it was fun!

This happened more than forty years ago. My excitement about learning and the joy of discovery has not abated. One of my life verses is Ecclesiastes 4:13 (NASB): "A poor yet wise lad is better than an old and foolish king who no longer knows how to receive instruction."

In spite of my gray hair, I still qualify as a poor but wise youth—the one without position, prestige, or power but who possesses wisdom. Becoming wise means becoming a learner. This is unlike the old and foolish king who no longer receives instruction. When leaders stop learning, we stop leading. I want to stay young by learning.

Back on the Tennis Court

Remember the tennis-practice illustration? We stand on the court of change. Each new ball thrown at us represents a new cultural or personal challenge. We keep swinging, seldom taking time to reflect on our swing, the speed of the ball, or the width of our stance. Reaction, not reflection, is the habit of the day. We keep swinging and we stop learning.

Author and business leader Peter Vaill describes this never-ending change as "permanent white water"—"the complex, turbulent, changing environment in which we are all trying to operate."[1] What's the proposed solution? Vaill writes, "Beyond all of the other new skills and attitudes that permanent white water requires, people have to be (or become) extremely effective learners."[2]

The everyday leader who doesn't know how to think, how to learn, "will be relentlessly shaped and influenced by the dominant culture around him or her."[3] Like others in our beleaguered culture, we become so busy doing that we stop learning. Busyness robs us of the skill to choose the good and the right.

Lifelong learners are leaders who know how to intentionally extract wisdom from life by employing a few simple tools. What does this life look like? Theologian J. I. Packer and author Carolyn Nystrom write that "the life of wisdom is a life of constant learning: constant evaluating, constant discerning, constant extension of one's understanding."[4]

Lifelong learning is not a passive dependence upon an expert—a learning mercenary—but a proactive choice to acquire wisdom from life. The wisdom path of experience becomes God's classroom for instruction. On this path, anyone can be a lifelong learner; it has nothing to do with age, classroom experience, or intelligence. Failed leaders are often failed learners who have failed the leadership test because they got caught in the white-water rapids of change and busyness.

There are few templates or formulas for life and ministry today.

We need godly wisdom—skillfully choosing the good and the right to bring people together to break new ground. This wisdom is acquired in life's classroom.

The Classroom of the Ordinary

I wake up every morning to go to class. I'm not pursuing a degree, auditing college classes, or enrolled in long-distance learning. My classroom is my life and ministry, what happens in the ordinary routines and rhythms of everyday life.

Much of life takes place in the ordinary. We look for flashes of the spectacular, but God delights in changing us through the ordinary—an offhand conversation, an unexpected experience, or an unseen choice of obedience. In his classic devotional book, *My Utmost for His Highest*, Oswald Chambers wrote, "We look for visions from heaven, for earthquakes and thunders of God's power . . . and we never dream that all the time God is in the commonplace things and people around us."[5]

The nineteenth-century poet Elizabeth Barrett Browning spoke of God's presence in the commonplace in this line from her poem *Aurora Leigh*.

Earth's crammed with heaven,
And every common bush afire with God:
But only he who sees, takes off his shoes;
The rest sit round it, and pluck blackberries.[6]

Our lives are "crammed with heaven" for those who take the time to slow down, pay attention, and learn. We discover that God shows up in the ordinary events of life—the "common bush[es] afire with God." This should not surprise us; the psalm-ist declares that there is nowhere he can go without God being present (Psalm 139:7-10).

C. S. Lewis wrote that "we may ignore, but we can nowhere evade, the presence of God. The world is crowded with Him. He walks everywhere incognito. And the incognito is not always hard to penetrate. The real labour is to remember, to attend. In fact, to come awake. Still more, to remain awake."[7]

This earthly life, crammed full of heaven life, where God walks incognito, is our classroom. The teacher is always present, but we can miss him if we're not awake, if we're sidetracked and spending our time "pluck[ing] blackberries." Like Jacob, we lament, "Surely the LORD is in this place, and I was not aware of it" (Genesis 28:16). When we miss his presence, we miss his wisdom.

Citing Proverbs 30:24-28, author Garry Friesen notes that one source of wisdom is "life itself." Life is the place where the Lord builds wisdom, and "we should become students of life as well as of Scripture."[8] Life is where transformation happens. Like Moses, our lives can be changed by a common bush filled with God's presence. Author Tish Harrison Warren writes, "God is forming us into a new people. And the place of that formation is in the small moments of today."[9]

In *The Quotidian Mysteries*—quotidian means "ordinary or everyday"—poet and novelist Kathleen Norris explains, "The ordi-nary activities I find most compatible with contemplation are walk-ing, baking bread, and doing laundry."[10] Why? Because God "loves us so much that the divine presence is revealed even in the meaning-less workings of everyday life. It is in the ordinary, the here and now, that God . . . desire[s] to be present to us in everything we do."[11]

Living this way requires intentionality, a discipline of paying attention to and learning from life. When everyday leaders see their quotidian experience as God's classroom for learning, they soon discover that education is more than attending conferences, listening to podcasts, or reading one more bestselling business book. Lifelong learners turn their lives and leadership settings into a classroom by paying attention to the "burning bush" of God's presence.

As everyday leaders, you and I are students in God's classroom of life. This classroom has no costly tuition, textbooks, or travel. It's available to everyone, anywhere, at any time. We quietly attend this classroom without fanfare or notice but with devotion and rapt attention. We daily "take off our shoes" and engage with the holy.

The Spotlight on Learning

Learning always implies that something is new to us. We learn new skills, information, values, or behaviors. When I'm learning something, I'm becoming different from what I once was: I know something new, I can perform a task I couldn't before, or I now see the importance of a certain value.

Lifelong learning includes all this and more. Being a disciple of Jesus means that I'm a special type of learner. The Greek word for *disciple* is *mathētēs*, which can be translated as "learner" or "follower."[12] The usage of this word in the New Testament departs from the typical secular usage of an apprentice or pupil and means following Christ so that one learns to "direct the whole of one's human existence toward the will of God."[13] This implies rejecting our old life and beginning the new life of following Christ (Ephesians 4:22-24). For disciples of Jesus, learning is a transformative experience in which we become more Christlike.

Learning, then, is the acquisition of godly wisdom—the ability to choose the good and the right—so that we can live as the ultimate learners, disciples of Jesus. My friend Randy Raysbrook calls this "deep learning."[14] Deep learning moves us beyond performance and information to the heart—where real life happens. After all, as Daniel Estes explains, "Wisdom works from the inside out to transform the entire person in the heart, which in Hebrew thought encompasses the intellect, the emotions and the will."[15] This type of deep learning shapes our hearts, minds, and wills to become more Christlike.

This deep learning is also lifelong. Not only do we learn *from* life but also we learn *for* life. Class is always in session. There's no diploma, certification, or graduation ceremony for the lifelong learner. This is a lifetime pursuit.

To summarize: Learning is an ongoing process of acquiring God's wisdom—the ability to do the good and the right—that deeply shapes our hearts, minds, and wills to be like Jesus. Lifelong learning is a mark of being a disciple of Jesus.

A Graduate Degree in Everyday Wisdom

After years of receiving bad haircuts, I decided to invest my money in a hair stylist. LaQuinta was my wife's stylist, so I made an appointment with her.[16] She proved to be a delightful person who also had an interest in life coaching. We quickly found some common ground.

While she was cutting my hair, we talked about coaching and learning. During one of our conversations, I had a sudden flash of inspiration. "You know, LaQuinta, this ten-by-ten salon is your classroom."

"I never thought of it this way, but you're right," she replied.

I began to ask her questions about what she had learned as a stylist since graduating from cosmetology school. It was obvious that she had moved beyond her basic classroom training. She described how her craft taught her about people and how to connect with them. She learned how good questions opened conversations. And dealing with the peculiarities and irregularities of her clients' hair gave her greater flexibility in her craft. She was schooled in this ten-by-ten salon.

LaQuinta's initial training provided basic skills that she adapted and changed as she worked with customers. She grew in wisdom that went beyond her training. If she were to mentor another stylist, she would probably say, "You know, they teach you this in the classroom, but this is how it works in real life." She acquired new wisdom through practice.

Researcher Donald Schön studied the professional lives of people like LaQuinta. He discovered that over time, quality professionals move from the step-by-step training of the classroom to a "knowing-in-action." This knowing-in-action is an intuitive professional knowledge and skill set that they do without thinking. This acquired and adapted wisdom is knowledge developed from experience, not formal training.[17]

LaQuinta is an example of someone who has knowing-in-action—wisdom from experience. A wealth of wisdom lies below the surface of her unconscious skills, waiting to be made explicit through reflection. My questions invited LaQuinta to reflect on this implicit knowledge—making the implicit explicit.

My questions encouraged her to think about, examine, and learn from these actions. When we reflect on our actions, "[we become] a researcher in the practice context."[18] This "reflection on action" finds wisdom buried in the action of our lives—a wisdom that lies dormant until we stop, think about it, and identify it in principled ways.[19]

Here's an interesting correlation. Did you know that *experience* and *expertise* have similar root meanings? *Experience*, which comes from Latin, means "knowledge or skill [gained] from doing, seeing, or feeling things."[20] The word *expert* also comes from Latin and means "a person wise from experience."[21] We become experts by learning from experience, by reflecting on our actions. But this takes work; expertise is not automatic.

Through experience, LaQuinta became an expert at both hair styling and customer relations. This implicit expertise was captured when she reflected on her experience—again, making the implicit explicit.

The salon was a greenhouse for wisdom's rapid growth. LaQuinta learned how to skillfully choose what is good for her customers—what will enrich their lives (and hair!). She also learned how to do what is right, providing services that are just and fair. God has used her everyday life experiences to grow wisdom.

Imagine the potential in a church or ministry if we were to teach people how to learn from God's presence in life's experiences! In our churches and ministries, we have experts in small group leadership, money management, effective parenting, and even the initiation of faith conversations with neighbors. When we lead as lifelong learners, we purposefully help people identify and unleash all this wisdom.

This everyday wisdom from life is not limited to a select few in a secret wisdom cult, graduates of prestigious universities, or the private domain of learning mercenaries. It's not confined to a religious place, such as a church or a temple; it's available in the busy public squares and streets (Proverbs 1:20-21). Lady Wisdom is found by lifelong learners, like hairstylists, everyday leaders who chase after her and listen to her voice. This pursuit can happen in something as ordinary as a hike in the country.

A Pathway for Lifelong Learning

> I passed by the field of a sluggard,
>   by the vineyard of a man lacking sense,
> and behold, it was all overgrown with thorns;
>   the ground was covered with nettles,
>   and its stone wall was broken down.
> Then I saw and considered it;
>   I looked and received instruction.
> A little sleep, a little slumber,
>   a little folding of the hands to rest,
> and poverty will come upon you like a robber,
>   and want like an armed man.
>
> PROVERBS 24:30-34, ESV

Lifelong learning starts with a casual country hike. While walking you spot a field overgrown with thorns and weeds and notice the farm buildings in disrepair. You could keep walking, but you choose to **stop**. This random scene becomes a learning opportunity. You're now in God's classroom. This is Browning's "bush afire," and it catches your attention.

What do you do in God's classroom? You stop to look and receive instruction. Stopping forces you to attentively look. A quick glance is not sufficient. You scan the area and notice its rundown condition. You become curious and want to **explore** what you see by asking some questions.

Out of curiosity you begin to wonder, *What's going on here? Why is the area overgrown? Why did the owner of the property not care for this land?* You think not only about the questions but also about the Scriptures. *How does the Bible address the situation? How can I think in an applicatory way?*

From this process of stopping and exploring, you learn a vital life lesson: "A little sleep, a little slumber, . . . and poverty will come upon you like a robber." If you're wise, you will record or **save** this lesson so that it's not forgotten.

But saving an insight doesn't make you any wiser. **Doing** or applying what you've saved makes information transformative. Jesus said it well: "If you . . . don't work [my words] into your life, you are like a stupid carpenter who built his house on the sandy beach" (Matthew 7:26, MSG). This is where "deep learning" happens. We work God's lessons into our lives through application.

Any pathway or road has markers to keep us pointed in the right direction. These markers help us locate where we are and where we are going. The Lifelong Learning Pathway has four markers on the way to wisdom: stopping, exploring, saving, and doing. When we follow the markers, we turn everyday routines into learning opportunities. Earth really is "crammed with heaven." There's splendor in the ordinary for those who are looking.

Practicing the Pathway Markers

Marker No. 1: Stop
In the rapid-fire pace of today's workplaces, neighborhoods, and ministry settings, everyday leaders must resist the pull toward non-stop activity. We must deliberately stop and reflect on how God is

at work in us, around us, and through us. Everyday leaders must practice stopping and thinking.

I've spent a good part of my life walking dogs. The Mowry family has always had a dog, and it was my duty to exercise our canine friends. Dog walking gave me time to think and pause from my busy routine. My mind was free to wander wherever I wanted it to go.

Sometimes my wandering mind didn't pay attention to what was going on around me. On my walks I would pass neighbors working in their yards.

When I walked past one neighbor, I made the obligatory comment, "How are you doing?"

He replied, "Not so good today."

It was two blocks later that I realized what he had said! I missed his honest response because I was so caught up in my own mental gymnastics. I missed the cue for a deeper conversation and a potential encounter designed by the Holy Spirit. I was not paying attention.

When we stop, we choose to provide ourselves with enough unhurried time that we can be attentive to the voice of God. Agrarian philosopher and author Wendell Berry writes that "as speed increases, care declines. . . . We know that there is a limit to the capacity of attention, and that the faster we go the less we see."[22] When we stop to look, we stop to care. Stopping means deciding to create time to reflect.

Did you know that the average visitor to an art gallery spends only twenty-seven seconds looking at a work of art?[23] According to author Winifred Gallagher, "attention" encourages the type of experience that is "beautifully described by the old-fashioned term 'rapt'—completely absorbed, engrossed, fascinated, perhaps even 'carried away'—that underlies life's deepest pleasures."[24] I too quickly rush by a painting or a needy neighbor. Speed robs me of fascination and pleasure.

God expects that we will stop, look at, and think about the world that surrounds us. Proverbs repeatedly challenges us with statements like "You lazy fool, look at an ant. Watch it closely; let it teach you a thing or two" (Proverbs 6:6, MSG). In other words, we're to think about what we see and from our observations draw conclusions about how to live.

Looking is so important for spiritual growth that there are around thirty different words in the Bible for noticing what is occurring around us. These words include *look*, *see*, *appear*, *behold*, *watch*, *examine*, *explore*, *peer*, *search*, *observe*, and *recognize*. You can begin looking in two easy steps:

1. Set aside time to look. After a busy day or week, sit back and mentally review the day's or week's events. Recall a significant conversation, a work conflict or success, time playing with your children, a Bible study you led, or a political event.

2. From this life scan, select an event or conversation to explore in depth. You're now ready for the next step: exploration.

Marker No. 2: Explore

Stopping to look around you is just the beginning. Exploration yields the real treasure. Exploration involves the hard work of thinking and asking good questions. Solomon warns us of what can happen if we fail to stop and think:

Lady Wisdom goes out in the street and shouts. . . .
"How long will you refuse to learn? . . .

> I'm ready to tell you all I know.
> As it is, I've called, but you've turned a deaf ear;
> I've reached out to you, but you've ignored me."
> (Proverbs 1:20, 24-25, MSG)

We stop to explore because this may be a Spirit-given *kairos* moment. There are two main Greek words for *time*—*chronos* and *kairos*. *Chronos* is typically "clock" time—chronological time. *Kairos* often indicates the "right time" or the "right moment." Author Henri Nouwen described *kairos* as "God's time" and said it "has to do with opportunity and fullness of meaning, moments that are ripe for their intended purpose."[25] It's what teachers refer to as "teachable moments." This is a Holy Spirit–generated moment to learn, and it can happen in the everyday routine of life.

We explore and think about these *kairos* moments by exercising the spiritual discipline of curiosity. In her book *A Curious Faith*, Lore Ferguson Wilbert writes: "Curiosity is a discipline of the spiritual sort, and it begins by asking some simple questions. . . . The Bible is a permission slip for those with questions. All these questions [in the Bible] aren't just pointing to *answers*. They're also saying, it's *okay to ask questions*. Asking questions is part of the Christian life."[26]

Jesus invited people to explore and think with him. He asked more than three hundred questions in the Gospels. He didn't ask questions to collect information; after all, he knew what was in people's hearts (John 2:24-25). He asked questions not for himself but for others. He wanted to challenge his followers to think and to learn.

Exploring and thinking with questions are forms of meditation. Poet and author Luci Shaw wrote that "meditation is much like contemplation; it attempts to approach the truth beneath the surface, to penetrate to the centre (*media* means middle) of things."[27] Exploring and thinking is the route to the "centre of things."

Asking questions is the basis of lifelong learning. Once you've learned to ask questions—relevant, appropriate, and substantial questions—you've learned how to learn.

Check out the training exercises for lifelong learning in the appendix (pages 163–164). You will find a list of helpful questions to aid you in your exploration.

Our exploration should not be done in a vacuum of our own experiences or opinions. We explore and think by searching the Scriptures. Life is not infallible. We can arrive at erroneous conclusions—such as deciding that the earth is flat—by observation alone. We must learn to think as Jesus thought, using the Scriptures as the filter and ultimate authority in our conclusions. Remember, experience is only one of the three pathways to wisdom; fixed commands and principled thinking are the other two paths.

Here are two questions to help us think with the mind of Christ:

1. What Bible event or person can instruct me in this life event?
2. Are there any biblical commands or principles I need to obey as I think about this event?

Marker No. 3: Save

Now is when learning happens; now is when wisdom is generated. We have identified a *kairos* moment in our lives. We have stopped and looked, explored and thought. We've squeezed out a lesson from experience. The Holy Spirit has brought this event and our insights concerning it to mind, and we don't want to miss this learning opportunity.

Harvesting and saving life's everyday wisdom means taking time to not only think about what we're learning but also write it down. Mary, the mother of Jesus, understood the value of saving life lessons. Thinking about her Son's life, she "treasured all these things in her heart" (Luke 2:51). Author Jan Johnson observes that Mary "kept . . . these [things] in mind just as people store treasures in a scrapbook and pore over them for years to come."[28] What a wonderful picture of saving.

A helpful habit for saving is to keep a learning journal. Journaling does more than chronicle our actions; it opens up and explores how God is working in our lives. Author Kirsten Birkett has found that "writing out what happened [in life] . . . forces me to look at my behaviour, at my feelings at the time and now, and examine it all in the light of what I know from Scripture. . . . I learn more about how to follow God. That's how I learn godliness."[29]

It's important to remember that a learning journal is different from a diary. Journals are not a record of day-to-day events or a form of Bible study. A learning journal is a personal, unique approach to collecting God's wisdom from life. Effective journaling happens when we

- purchase an inexpensive journal;
- write without regarding grammar or punctuation;
- draw or illustrate what we're learning, thinking, or feeling; and
- capture our learning lessons in one- or two-sentence principles.

Our learning journal becomes a treasure chest of discoveries that reveal how God works through life. The wisdom recorded can shape conversations and teaching opportunities and provide insight to those we're mentoring or discipling.

In a learning journal we not only process what we're learning but also capture and save a principle or insight learned. We could call these principles *maxims*. Maxims are proverbial in nature, not meant to be universal laws but concise statements that make the learning memorable. The goal is to state one new insight or principle in a brief, memorable sentence. Here are some examples:

- Life must be limited to be invested.
- Character trumps competency.
- It can't think; don't let it outfox you.
- I must choose to be still in order to be ready.

My mentor, John Ed, had some great life maxims. These include:

- Sometimes when we give people the benefit of the doubt, the doubt's not really a benefit.
- There's always an exception to the rule, but you can't make the exception the rule.

Marker No. 4: Do

We live out our harvested wisdom when we apply it in practical and meaningful ways. Without this step, we miss out on God's blessing (James 1:25). Living out everyday wisdom could mean stopping to pray, changing an attitude, thinking differently about a person, doing a good deed, or starting a conversation. Jan Johnson exhorts us to "train ourselves never to walk away from Scripture without responding."[30] I think the same could be said of life lessons.

One suggestion for living out the wisdom gleaned from life is to use your imagination to picture how life could be different if you applied this wisdom. What could happen if you applied this truth within the next twenty-four hours? With whom could you share this lesson?

A Final Reflection: Lifelong Learners Leave an Inheritance

My parents left my sisters and me few possessions when they passed away. Dad and Mom lived modestly, so their estate was meager. What they left to their children revealed what they valued.

One item I received was Dad's set of William Barclay's Daily Study Bible series, commentaries on the New Testament. I found the books filled with Dad's notes, underlinings, and questions. He interacted with the text, challenging his mind to explore and expand its understanding. Gleaning wisdom from the Bible was a supreme value in his life.

My dad came to faith later in life.[31] He had only a high school education and no advanced training. He worked hard at studying the Bible. In the margins of Barclay's books, I discovered an inquisitive spirit and a hunger to learn. What a priceless heritage!

The second item I received was a file folder of Dad's Sunday school notes. He taught an adult class at his little country church for twenty years. In reviewing his class notes, I noticed the number of questions he asked the class. My father invited people to be learners by asking them questions. Dad's questions reflected his personal commitment to learn.

Dad and mom were everyday leaders whose lives exemplified Ecclesiastes 4:13. Although Dad was a gray-haired senior rather than a "poor but wise youth," he was willing to receive instruction. The only power and prestige he had was a life of wisdom gained from experience. He kept on learning until dementia clouded his mind. Learning was a heritage he passed on to me.

Everyday leaders must be lifelong learners. We must learn from the Scriptures and from life. Learning is an intentional and purposeful action; it's not haphazard or delegated to someone else. Lifelong learners are able to gain everyday wisdom that empowers them to bring people together to break new ground—to develop fresh, biblical, and practical approaches to meet local challenges. We must learn how to learn.

A Case Study in Lifelong Learning

Every day I step into God's classroom—he's the teacher, I'm the pupil, and life is the classroom. I can count on his instruction to be both unpredictable and surprising. Take my "Bulgarian epiphany."

For several years, I visited Bulgaria to assist our Navigator missionaries in their ministry to pastors and churches. During one visit, I was asked to speak on disciplemaking at an evangelical seminary. I was thrilled at the opportunity.

How can you start your journey as a lifelong learner? In the appendix is a training exercise for lifelong learning. Consider setting aside time soon to complete this exercise.

The director of the seminary asked me to teach from my book *The Ways of the Alongsider*. At the heart of the book is the importance of relational disciplemaking.

I was about sixty minutes into my first session when a Bulgarian student raised his hand and asked a question: "Bill, you say disciplemaking is all about relationships and not about information. You say Jesus taught from life and not a classroom. Yet here we are in a classroom being lectured about disciplemaking. There seems to be a disconnect here. Why is that?"

I immediately thought, *That's a good question!* I then did what all good speakers do when surprised: I muttered a half-hearted answer and kept going with my lecture.

With plenty of time to think on the flight home, my mind went back to this student's observation. I **stopped** to think about what had happened.

What was behind the student's dissonance between what he was feeling and my teaching method and lesson? I began to **explore** how I felt about what happened. I discovered I was a little embarrassed. The student had made a good point. He was making a legitimate observation that needed some answers.

My mind asked more questions. Soon, the phrase *The medium is the message* popped into my head. This saying is a very succinct form of the late Canadian philosopher Marshall McLuhan's critique of contemporary communication. Sometimes the medium (video, television, lecture, discussion, etc.) we choose can obscure or overshadow the message we're trying to send. In many cases, the medium itself becomes the message.[32]

I was teaching on the importance of relationships, yet the medium (a classroom lecture) overshadowed the message (relational disciplemaking). The dissonance happened because the medium became the message, which implied that disciplemaking happens by lecture in a classroom. No wonder the student felt a disconnect. This was an aha moment for me, an epiphany or illuminating discovery about learning and teaching.

Now I understood why many pastors and churches fail to

grasp relational disciplemaking. Most pastors are trained in a seminary or classroom setting. Almost unconsciously, they adopt the medium of the lecture as the message for how to disciple others. No wonder our churches are filled with classrooms, pulpits, and lecterns.

What's the message we're sending by the medium we choose? Disciplemaking happens in a classroom with an appointed teacher or expert. The medium of the classroom has now become the message we're sending about how to disciple others. The medium I choose must complement rather than compete with or even overshadow the message I'm sending.

I mentally **saved** that principle and began to explore how to apply it. I soon had an opportunity to **do** what I had learned. I was asked to lead a workshop on question asking at a training conference. I wanted to send the message that questions are important for learning and growth. What medium or teaching method could best accomplish this?

I decided to lead the workshop by only asking questions. I would not lecture or make any statements other than to summarize what others said. To teach the importance of asking questions, I would model asking questions! The medium would become the message.

I went into the session fearful of failure—I had never done anything like this before. I came away thrilled—we had a rich time, and participants shared some insights that were better than mine. They experienced the power of asking questions in a setting designed around questions.

My Bulgarian epiphany was a wisdom-creating moment. This simple lesson changed how I think about training and teaching. I now ask myself, *How does my teaching strategy (the medium) enhance and contribute to the lesson (the message)?* I must ensure that the medium and the message are in sync with one another.

This insight started in Bulgaria with a question by a seminary student. You can never predict when the Lord will turn everyday life into a classroom for learning.

The Way of Collaboration

Everyday leaders capture the power of people working together.

The ministry of the church is not the responsibility
of a few professionals; it is the divine responsibility
of every one of us.

WAYNE CORDEIRO, *DOING CHURCH AS A TEAM*

INTERVIEWING PROSPECTIVE STAFF for our regional Navigators
staff team was always a collaborative process. As was our custom,
the team met prior to the interview to discuss the questions we
would ask the applicant. We identified the usual ones: "What are
your strengths?" "Tell us about your past ministries," and "What
is your ideal working situation?" One question, though, jumped
out from all the rest.

"If you could describe yourself as a cartoon character, which
character would you choose and why?" was Dean's question. We
all laughed at first, dismissing the question as an attempt to bring
some levity to a serious experience.

But then I took a second look. *How would I answer the question?*

I asked myself. (Seriously, I did ask myself—and the job applicant—this question! Never let a good question go unanswered.)

Who was my cartoon character? My mind jumped to Mighty Mouse, a 1960s cartoon hero that I watched as a kid. Mighty Mouse was a cross between Mickey Mouse and Superman. This tiny mouse had big ears, a cape, and tights that covered a muscular little frame. His triumphant cry to action was "Here I come to save the day!"

Mighty Mouse could vanquish any villain, lift any vehicle, and fly like an eagle. Who *wouldn't* aspire to be as powerful as Mighty Mouse? For years, my picture of leadership was found in Mighty Mouse. As I think back on my ministry experiences, however, I realize that seldom does one person have the power and ability to save the day. A strong team, however, can possess the superpowers to find the right solutions to any challenge. Effective teams bring people together to break new ground.

The Mighty Mouse Effect

I faced the biggest challenge of my young Navigators career when I directed a summer program in Columbus, Ohio. We gathered sixty students to live in a fraternity house and a sorority house for two months for work, Bible study, and discipleship. I was above my pay grade managing all the drama that comes with two houses of nineteen- to twenty-one-year-olds. I needed wisdom. The Lord used the staff team to save the day. Together we created a Mighty Mouse effect.

We believed the Lord had brought us together to lead this program. There was a synergy, confidence, and commitment that I had never experienced before. I had the director title, but the summer program didn't rise or fall on my leadership. The team was the leader.

Each staff person contributed wisdom I didn't possess, related to students in ways I could not, and dealt with crises beyond my experience. We colabored—collaborated—and the program was better for it. I wasn't alone. I was better with others. Deep learning had happened in my life.

What is collaborative leadership? Sally Nash, Jo Pimlott, and Paul Nash, in *Skills for Collaborative Ministry*, write that collaboration "brings an energy and synergy to what we do and enables us to achieve something we could never have done alone."[1] This ability to "achieve something we could never have done alone" is the Mighty Mouse effect.

That summer in Ohio, I realized that I didn't have to be the omnicompetent leader—the one who was skilled in everything. I could mix my leadership gifting with the competencies and personalities of the other leaders. We were better together than apart. Mighty Mouse became a symbol for our team: We worked together to save the day. Our collective wisdom shaped our decisions. Collaborative leadership is the key to bringing people together to break new ground.

There are a variety of leadership styles and practices that best serve specific needs. Collaborative leadership is one of many styles and is most appropriate when one or more of these conditions are present:

- *A big challenge is encountered.* Big challenges can't be solved by one leader. The wisdom of many is needed to address the challenge.

- *A new approach is required.* Collaboration brings a creative power to develop new ideas, approaches, and practices.

- *Nothing is working.* Collaborative leadership recognizes that when current business or ministry forms (approaches, resources, tools) aren't working, we must wisely create new ones.

- *Ownership is needed.* Collaboration believes that the greater the participation, the greater the ownership. Solitary leaders must move from the Sinai model of Moses' solo leadership to a partnership with others.

When these needs coalesce, a collaborative approach is the most effective in creating the wisdom needed for new solutions. Collaboration brings people together to break new ground.

Collaboration Starts with a Blank Piece of Paper

Let's make some basic distinctions about collaboration.

First, collaboration is not *coordination*. Coordination simply means that we talk together about the best dates and resources, coordinating times and application. Second, collaboration is not *cooperation*. In cooperation, we're sensitive to one another's goals, resources, and schedules so that we're not in competition with one another—a competition that could doom one or both of us. Collaboration includes coordination and cooperation, but it's something more.

In *Collaborative Leadership*, David Chrislip and Carl Larson describe collaboration as "a mutually beneficial relationship between two or more parties who work toward common goals by sharing responsibility, authority, and accountability for achieving results."[2] I agree with that definition, but let's make it simpler: Collaboration starts with a blank piece of paper.

To engage in true collaboration, we need collaborative leaders who don't have a plan in mind, a proposal to promote, or a solution for the situation. The collaborative leader comes with a blank piece of paper, a practical process, and an invitation for others to join him or her in creating a solution together.

Collaborative leadership is the art of helping people work together to accomplish a commonly owned goal or vision in a way that promotes equal ownership and equal contribution.

Collaboration happens when a ministry or life challenge becomes so important or complex that one person doesn't have all the wisdom to meet it. New ground must be broken that requires a new way of leading. Too often, our working assumption is that a solitary leader provides the answers and direction. This solitary leadership style has dominated our leadership thinking and practice since the days of Moses.

As he led Israel to the Promised Land, Moses was the policeman, the judge, and the jury to this fledgling nation. Then along came his father-in-law. When Jethro observed Moses in action, he made an insightful judgment:

> What is this you are doing for the people? Why do you
> alone sit as judge, while all these people stand around you
> from morning till evening? . . . What you are doing is not
> good. You and these people who come to you will only
> wear yourselves out. The work is too heavy for you; you
> cannot handle it alone. (Exodus 18:14, 17-18)

Moses suffered from the disease of omnicompetency. He needed to delegate to a team, or he would wear himself out and the people with him. He couldn't handle leading alone.

Keith Sawyer writes that "we're drawn to the image of the lone genius whose mystical moment of insight changes the world. But the lone genius is a myth; instead, it's group genius that generates breakthrough innovation."[3] What was Jethro's suggestion? He instructed Moses to select leaders "over thousands, hundreds, fifties and tens" (Exodus 18:21) rather than continue as a solitary leader. Many were to carry the load.

Like Moses, we can be solitary leaders coming down from the mountain—or out of an office—with a plan to enter the Promised Land expecting people to follow us. The solitary leader asks, "Did you get the memo?" Instead, what we should be asking is "How can we work together?"

Collaboration Is Biblical

"From one cover of the Bible to the other, the Creator of the universe works as a team," write Ryan Hartwig and Warren Bird.[4] This thread of collaboration is woven into the Bible's narrative.

The "team" of the Trinity worked together in creating humankind in "our image" (Genesis 1:26). This same Trinity was present at Jesus' baptism (Mark 1:10-11). The Trinity commissions us to make disciples (Matthew 28:19) and brings about our salvation (Ephesians 1:4-6, 17). The Bible presents the Trinitarian nature of God as a model of teamwork.

Sally Nash, Jo Pimlott, and Paul Nash note that "a fundamental argument for collaborative ministry is that God collaborates with us and that this is the pattern we are offered in the New Testament."[5] This pattern of collaboration marked the ministry of the apostle Paul.

We often picture Paul as the rugged individualist who moved forward with determination and faith without regard to whether others joined him. The biblical record shows something different. In nearly every place that Paul is mentioned in Acts, he's accompanied by people (see 13:2–14:23; 16:6, 11, 25; 18:1-4; 20:4-6). He called them "fellow workers" implying equal ownership or partnership (Romans 16:3, 7, 9, 12, ESV). He valued each person's service or function (1 Corinthians 3:5; Colossians 4:7-9), freeing them to minister from their distinctive giftings (1 Corinthians 3:6, 9). The apostle collaborated with people without regard to gender, culture, or ethnic differences (Galatians 3:28; Colossians 4:14-17).

At the end of his life, Paul was wrongly accused and sat in jail waiting for a trial. He was discouraged by the desertion of fickle friends (2 Timothy 4:10) and joyfully welcomed Onesiphorus as a friend who "often refreshed" him (1:16). There are hints of loneliness when Paul instructed Timothy to come to him soon (4:9), to bring Mark, who was "helpful" to him (4:11), and to bring his cloak and parchments (4:13).

Paul longed for his ministry collaborators to be with him. He did not want to live or die alone. Paul needed partners until the end.

Collaboration Is Faith-Filled

Starting with a blank sheet of paper is an act of faith. We're saying, "Lord, we're laying aside our agendas and preferences and trusting you to give us wisdom to create something new by working together." The Old Testament patriarch Abraham illustrates trusting God to create what doesn't exist.

Abraham was asked by God to sacrifice his son Isaac (Genesis 22:2). This was a heart-wrenching step for a loving father; additionally, God's covenant was tied up with Isaac (Genesis 17:2-8).

Abraham's blessing to be a "father of many nations" flowed through Isaac: No son, no blessing.

How was God going to fulfill his promise when he asked Abraham to eliminate the promise bearer? The answer to this dilemma is found in Romans 4:17-18: "As it is written, 'I have made you the father of many nations'—in the presence of the God in whom he believed, who gives life to the dead and calls into existence the things that do not exist" (ESV).

Abraham resolved the tension by trusting God to do one of two things: either raise Isaac from the dead or create another sacrifice that did not exist. God did the latter; he called into existence that which hadn't existed—a sacrificial ram caught in a bush (Genesis 22:13).

Collaboration is an act of faith, of believing God to call into existence something that doesn't exist; he fills in the blank page of paper as we seek him and work together. Faith allows us to lay aside our preferences and agendas and trust God to create something new.

The Marks of a Collaborative Leader

When we mention collaborative leadership, some of us head for the door! We picture collaboration as people working in a committee, constantly talking and meeting without any decisions. For those of us who like action, we shiver at this prospect. *Who's leading this charade?* We look around the table and point to the person designated as the "facilitator."

Facilitative leaders can exemplify all that's wrong with collaboration; they are the antithesis of the solitary leader. The stereotype is that facilitators are really nonleaders—sponsoring endless conversations, drinking lots of coffee, leading people nowhere. Who wants this type of leadership?

Collaborative leadership is different from this stereotype. Four qualities mark collaborative leaders: They are focused, they practice and expect the Great Surrender, they engage everyone, and they take action. Let's explore these qualities a little more.

Collaborative leaders **are focused**; they're single-minded about the process but hands-off on the outcomes. After all, we're calling people together around a blank piece of paper to capture their wisdom to create solutions for issues that none of us could solve by ourselves. Collaborative leaders passionately and intentionally guide the process but allow the solutions to emerge from the group. They purposefully lead from a commitment to indifference.

Collaborative leaders **practice and expect the Great Surrender.** This means asking people to suspend their agendas and preferences and trust God to create something new, to fill in that blank piece of paper.

Collaborative leaders **engage everyone** in the problem-solving process and the creation of a practical strategy. They draw upon the wisdom of each member, realizing that as a solitary person, they do not possess all the answers. Collaborative leaders wear the hat of a facilitator.

True facilitative leaders believe there's wisdom in the community and diligently work at extracting this wisdom through questions, patient listening, and summarizing. Facilitation also means delegating responsibility and tasks to each team member. This is a collective enterprise, not the work of a solitary individual. This is true facilitation.

Collaborative leaders want to **take action.** They're not interested in sponsoring more meetings for discussion. Meetings are simply tools for collaboration, not permanent events. Their first priority is creating practical strategies for action. If there's no ultimate action or strategy, then leadership has failed. Action results when leaders choose proactivity over passivity.

Let's Take a Collaboration Audit

When the situation requires collaborative leadership, how would you assess your ability to lead collaboratively? Using a scale of 1 to 5, with 1 being the lowest and 5 the highest, rate yourself on the following:

_____ 1. I involve those most affected by a decision in the decision-making process.

_____ 2. I'm more committed to the process than to my view of the outcome.

_____ 3. I freely and intentionally share information relevant to the issue or problem.

_____ 4. I view people as equal contributors rather than people to whom I delegate responsibility.

_____ 5. I take time to build relationships with each team member.

_____ 6. I'm willing to suspend my preferences or goals in order to create a new solution.

_____ 7. I intentionally identify people's strengths and look for ways to draw them into the creative decision-making process.

_____ 8. I ask a lot of questions rather than giving answers or instructions.

_____ 9. I ask questions to draw out meanings and values from others.

_____ 10. I make it a practice not to make any decisions unless they've been shaped and discussed by each member.

Answer the questions below to assess what you've learned from this collaboration audit?

1. What did you discover about your collaborative skills?

2. What collaborative strengths/areas of growth did you identify?

Collaboration Requires the Great Surrender

My friend Chip Weiant wrote in an article on "uncommon sense" that "people intentionally choose to unite—or divide—every day. What is less understood is that their choice is determined by a lack of character not by a lack of competency."[6]

Interview any human resource director or missions leader, and they will tell you that most workplace or ministry problems and dismissals are not issues of competency but issues of character. Whether the setting is in a church or business, people have a hard time working together if character is not present. Character always trumps competency. Just ask Pastor Dale.

Dale invited me into his church to help his congregation build a disciple-making culture. We worked at building a team but were blindsided by some members' resistance to the process. Meetings ended in debates, conversations yielded complaints, and decisions were second-guessed. It got so bad that an ad hoc committee began meeting to develop an alternate strategy—without including the pastor!

After a year of trying to work with this church, I decided that I could go no further. To my disappointment, and Dale's discouragement, I decided to stop my ministry to this church. This group's influence was too widespread to compete against.

It was obvious that this group had their own picture and agenda of where the church should go. There was little evidence of the mind of Christ and the character that follows. This group of people had not made the Great Surrender.

The Great Surrender means doing the Father's will above our own. Jesus modeled the Great Surrender when he stated, "My food is to do the will of him who sent me and to finish his work" (John 4:34). In John 17:4, he concluded his ministry by saying to the Father, "I glorified you on earth, having accomplished the work that you gave me to do" (ESV).

You may be thinking, *Jesus is an obvious example of the Great Surrender. After all, he's the Son of God.*

Where else do we find the Great Surrender lived out in Scripture? Another example is the apostle Paul's protégé Timothy.

In the book of Philippians, Paul describes what theologians call the kenosis of Christ—emptying himself to become a man (2:6-8). Paul took Jesus' act of emptying himself and showed how it was illustrated in the character of his friend Timothy, who was like a son to him:

> For I have no one like him, who will be genuinely
> concerned for your welfare. For they all seek their
> own interests, not those of Jesus Christ. But you
> know Timothy's proven worth, how as a son with
> a father he has served with me in the gospel.
> (2:20-22, ESV)

What can we observe about the Great Surrender in Timothy's example? We must become what theologian Homer Kent calls people "of equal soul."[7] This is what Paul meant when he stated that "I have no one like [Timothy]"—no one of equal soul. Timothy shared Paul's heart and chose to be concerned more for the welfare and interests of others than for his own personal agenda. J. A. Motyer notes that to "be genuinely anxious for your welfare" means that Timothy was "naturally and genuinely pains-taking" in his concern for the Philippians' welfare.[8]

Jesus' priorities were Timothy's priorities. Timothy made some choices to subordinate himself to the Lord and to the apostle Paul. "Serving in the gospel" could also be translated "slaved for the gospel." The Great Surrender means we always choose second place. Motyer comments, "Timothy's subordinate place is clear. In terms of slavery, he was a second-class slave. His task was to be a second-in-command. And he was ready for it to be so. He never usurped."[9]

We make the Great Surrender when we wave the white flag, surrendering our personal agendas and preferences in order to seek the Lord's best as a team gathers together. This white flag of surrender is epitomized by a blank sheet of white paper—a page devoid of ideas, agendas, and time lines.

How does the Great Surrender start? With two acts of prayer. The first prayer is what author Ruth Haley Barton calls "the prayer for indifference." "In this prayer we ask God to work in our hearts to make us indifferent to anything but the will of God."[10] How the prayer for indifference is answered can be found in the example of Timothy.

The second prayer is a request for wisdom. The Lord invites us to seek him for wisdom (James 1:5). We're choosing to collaborate with others because the challenge is too big for one person to solve. We choose to fear God and stand small in his presence, needing his guidance and wisdom. Without his wisdom we can't untangle ourselves from some preconceived outcomes we consider the best. This is the mark of the Great Surrender.

Collaboration Needs a Game Plan

Analogies are funny things. What appeals to one person may be a turnoff to others. My wife sometimes tires of men sharing sports analogies. "It's such a guy thing," she says. However, one sports analogy has now entered into our common vocabulary: the game plan.

In sports, the game plan is the strategy a coach develops for each game. It's a unique plan to match the strengths and weaknesses of the opposing team. Game plans have entered our cultural language and have come to mean a simple plan of action, a strategy to accomplish a goal.

Collaborative leaders need a game plan in order to be effective. Five simple steps make up a collaborative leader's game plan: Select, pause, focus, explore, and plan. This game plan will help bring people together to break new ground.

Select

When I reached the wonderful age of seventy, I wrote down three simple maxims to guide me in this season of life. First, life is too short for more paperwork (hooray!). Second, life is too short for more upgrades. Whether it's for my computer or phone, I dislike spending the time to make one more upgrade to a system. Finally, life is too short to work with people with whom I have little chemistry.

Life has taught me that relational conflict is part of leadership; dealing with conflicts is one means of growth. But I can make choices about the people I want to team with in collaborative settings. Three qualities have guided how I choose who to work with.

Those we select to collaborate with should be people of character, contribution, and chemistry. First, they should be people of character who have embraced the Great Surrender; those who have waved the white flag of surrender to their own personal agendas to create something new. People of character are on a transformative journey of thinking and living as Jesus thought and lived.

Second, we should collaborate with people of contribution. Collaborative teams have a diversity of giftings, experiences, and personalities. The team can be as diverse as schoolteachers, business owners, ministry leaders, and stay-at-home moms. Collaborative teams need people from a variety of backgrounds and expertise so that we can pull from the diverse wisdom of the community. We also need people with different personality types, particularly extroverts and introverts. Author Susan Cain documents studies that show "the most effective teams are composed of a healthy mix of introverts and extroverts."[11] Introverts and extroverts bring strengths of personality that will make the team better.

Finally, we should select people we have chemistry with. Chemistry means that there's a potential to enjoy working together. Life is too short to spend time arguing endlessly, resolving personality conflicts, or dealing with rampant egos. While these challenges will happen in the best of teams, we can minimize them by choosing people we have chemistry with. Collaborative leaders should like and respect the people they team with.

How many people do you invite to join a team? I've found that groups of four to six people are the best size. There's a practical side to this: It's easier to coordinate people's schedules. Ryan Hartwig and Warren Bird offer this helpful insight: "Every person on a team doubles the team's communicative and collaborative complexity."[12] The larger the team, the more administration. Additionally, smaller teams encourage relationships and the free flow of discussion and ideas. People can't hide in a small group.

Collaborative teams are typically short-lived. They exist to address a current problem or challenge. Once an action plan is wisely generated, the team may dissolve.

Pause

Pausing is the prelude to collaboration. In my years of experience in leading teams, this step is the one I've tended to neglect or to implement in a dismissive manner. Once the team is selected, we must face the implications of the Great Surrender. We must wave the white flag of surrender to our preciously owned agendas and preferences. We need to pause before planning.

Here is a pausing assignment that can be completed individually or in a team setting:

1. Read and reflect on Philippians 2:19-24.

- What attitudes do you observe about Timothy's call to service?
- What do you think Timothy surrendered to serve as Paul's partner?
- How would you describe Timothy's motivation to serve?
- What one insight from Timothy's example can guide your participation on this team?

2. Reflect on and answer the following questions:

- What do you need to surrender to participate on this team? This could include expected outcomes, personal agendas or preferences, or a projected schedule. Write out your answer in detail.
- If the Lord is the head of this church or ministry, what will it look like to follow and submit to his leadership?
- How would you describe your contribution to this team? Identify your strengths, spiritual gifts, and experiences.
- What can help you contribute but not dominate in your contribution?

Focus

Collaboration is a team trusting God together to create that which doesn't exist. To be most effective, this creative act must be focused. The fast-charging tennis-ball challenge must be clearly articulated. Citing one study of more than five hundred leaders across thirty companies, Keith Sawyer notes that "unclear objectives became the biggest barrier to effective team performance."[13] Effective teams need a clear focus.

A clear focus or goal provides clarity of direction. It also fosters a sense of ownership; without ownership or urgency, commitment will be half-hearted. You can encourage ownership by asking two questions:

1. What would happen if we failed to address this problem or challenge?
2. How would you describe this challenge in your own words?

This second question is imperative. After asking team members to write the challenge in their own words, I invite them to share what they wrote. This allows me to hear whether everyone is on the same page. Paraphrasing the goal may yield new insights into the problem, making it clearer than it was before.

An important element of focusing is taking inventory of the challenge and the team. This means taking stock of the resources you have and identifying the contribution of each team member. I've discovered that identifying the primary contribution of each team member is the first priority, with an inventory of resources following. A simple assignment to identify contribution is to ask team members to describe their individual giftings or contributions. What does each member bring to the team setting?

The inventory of resources includes such practical subjects as budgeting, scheduling, the projected start-up date, and administrative assistance. These resources are necessary for the implementation of your strategy.

Taking an inventory reveals what's missing in education, training, knowledge, and implementation resources. These factors will help shape your game plan for collaboration.

Explore

Exploration starts with understanding the context or culture in which the problem or challenge is occurring. We will go into this in greater detail when we discuss what it means to gain cultural wisdom.

In the case study at the end of this chapter, I describe the design of a training initiative for Navigators staff. Prior to designing a solution, my team spent hours discussing our staff's ministry contexts. We discovered that our ministry culture often values initiative over competency. Telling was assumed to be teaching, working at one's own pace was more valued than conformity to process, and having access to training was more important than training-session attendance. Exploring our context shaped our ultimate outcomes.

Exploring the context focuses on the end user. We create a mental picture of who will be experiencing our strategy. What will they think, feel, and do when we put our plan into motion? How will this strategy help them succeed? Exploring our context means thinking with the end user in mind.

Exploring is the creative act of designing innovative solutions to a challenge or problem. We will examine several skills and practices for exploring in collaborative leadership in our chapter on ministry innovation.

Plan

Deciding on a plan of action is the most important part of the collaborative effort. My friend Brenda, a leadership coach, frequently comments that "until it's on the calendar, it's just another nice idea." Schedules propel us to action.

Everything up to this point is like a giant funnel. We start with lots of challenges, problems, and ideas; in fact, we probably have more good ideas than we know what to do with. The funnel is big but must now become narrow. We must decide what to do.

At this juncture we come back to our reference point: Are we thinking like Jesus? We must stop and ask ourselves before the Lord, *Will our strategy best accomplish God's purposes? Are our values and outcomes aligned with biblical values and outcomes? Have we prayed for indifference, setting aside our agendas for the greater good?*

Here are five simple questions the team members can ask themselves to guide the funneling process:

1. What action steps will best accomplish our original goal? Prioritize the ideas that best answer this question.
2. What solutions best take into consideration the context or culture of our ministry—the end user?
3. How will this strategy best accomplish our priorities and values?
4. Which strategy can be implemented in a speedy manner with the resources we have?
5. What action steps are most immediate to move our strategy forward?

Long before the explosion of Pixar cartoon movies, there was *Snow White*, the first feature-length cartoon movie. As Warren Bennis and Patricia Ward Biederman write in their book *Organizing Genius*, "*Snow White* was a dream with a deadline."[14] Walt Disney envisioned the finished product and built a team to accomplish his vision.

If we don't put deadlines next to our dreams and desires, they remain nice sentiments, and the world already has an abundance of nice sentiments. Collaborative leaders always move the process toward closure and action. Action happens when we answer some basic questions:

- *Who* is responsible for what?
- *What* are our immediate action goals?
- *Where* will our strategy take place?
- *When* will the deadlines be set?

- *Why* should this strategy be implemented?
- *How* will it be accomplished?

In the appendix you will find a training exercise on collaboration. Consider using it when you start your next collaborative venture.

How Does God Lead in the Collaborative Process?

The collaborative process has come to an end. From a logical point of view, your plan of action seems wise. However, is this plan the leading of God? How do we discern his voice in developing our plan of action?

Answering this question in a comprehensive way is beyond the scope of this book. Besides, others have addressed this question more eloquently than I (two excellent books with different perspectives are *Hearing God* by Dallas Willard and *God's Will* by J. I. Packer and Carolyn Nystrom). But I have learned four principles that can give a partial answer to this question of God's leading.

1. *He leads as we share the mind of Christ.* My wife, Peggy, can usually predict what I will say or do. After forty-plus years of marriage, she knows how I think and what I value.

   Philosopher and author Dallas Willard makes a similar observation in discerning God's guidance: "Jesus calls us friends if we do what he commands (Jn 15:14). . . . Friends are people who understand one another, and so as friends of Jesus we obey because we understand what God, our intimate Friend, is doing."[15]

   Friends implicitly know what the other thinks and values.

As friends of God, we learn what he thinks and values as the Scriptures saturate our lives. We develop the mind of Christ when the Bible becomes our second language. We learn to naturally think his thoughts and act according to his will because out of love, we want to please him.

2. *He leads through insights and discoveries.* In working collaboratively with others, there's usually a moment when a breakthrough happens. Someone has a new insight, makes a new discovery, or brings in a different point of view. An aha moment happens. Time after time I have seen a quick consensus form when this "aha" happens. My teasing quote at this point is "Flesh and blood has not revealed this to you" (Matthew 16:17, ESV)! The Holy Spirit brought an insight that shapes our strategy.

3. *He leads through a Bible-inspired process.* The game plan for collaboration is a Bible-inspired process, meaning that it's shaped by biblical principles and focuses on God-honoring outcomes. Please note that it is Bible-inspired and not "inspired by God." I don't claim that the Lord revealed this process to me in a special revelation, but I will argue that the Scriptures inspired it by example and principle.

4. *He leads through "the sound of a low whisper"* (1 Kings 19:12, ESV). This is the still, small voice of God that I, and others, have experienced at times. Sometimes his voice is like a whispering in my heart. Other times the Spirit highlights a passage or key words from Scripture. Sometimes it's through the words of a friend.

However we describe it, there's a distinct impression

that the Holy Spirit is speaking to us in a personal and direct way. While this "low whisper" should be listened to, we must be careful about giving it an authoritative position in a group setting like collaboration. Just as we're to "test the spirits" (1 John 4:1), so we should humbly test the whisper of God when it comes to a group decision. Prayer, discussion, wisdom from mature believers, and an ultimate consensus from the group will decide whether this word from God is to be applied personally or is a directive for the group's strategic decisions.

The Holy Spirit is present in all these principles, weaving his way through each, leading us to wisely decide what is the good and right thing to do. There is no mechanical formula. At times, some principles may be more dominant than others. When we employ the mind of Christ, we can discern the appropriate application at the appropriate time.

A Final Reflection: Collaboration Arises in Unusual Places

Solitary leaders are like the myth of solitary artists; sometimes the reality is something different. Did you know that the great Renaissance artists were products of workshops and apprenticeships? Dozens of artists assisted Michelangelo in painting the Sistine Chapel ceiling. Van Gogh and Gauguin prodded each other to greatness and helped launch the Impressionist movement in art. Picasso and Braque shared a studio and transformed twentieth-century painting. The songwriting partnerships of Lerner and Loewe, Leiber and Stoller, or Lennon and McCartney illustrate collaborative songwriting. C. S. Lewis and J. R. R. Tolkien collaborated to create enduring literary classics.

The award-winning chef and author Alice Waters writes that "teams of people working together always create something that's better and richer and more interesting than what a single chef can accomplish on their own."[16] Even cooking demonstrates the principle that collaboration draws on the wisdom of the many to create that which is new.

Our Lord wants us to work together. Everyday leaders believe that collaboration is inherent in the Trinity and should be practiced in the church. Collaboration is an act of stewarding the wisdom found in the community of believers. I believe that when the occasion demands it, the Lord will use people committed to the Great Surrender and a blank piece of paper to create something that doesn't exist. Everyday leaders practice collaboration by bringing people together to break new ground.

Ready to start leading in collaborative ways? Read through the training exercise in the appendix. Identify a local challenge that needs a strategy. Practice the steps in the exercise and bring people together to break new ground.

A Case Study in Collaboration

The Navigators Church Ministries (NCM) national leadership team presented me with a challenge: create a training process for our one hundred full- and part-time staff scattered across the US, a process that would take into consideration the limitations of funding and time.

This challenge put a bit of the fear of God into my soul. I had questions but no answers; I had preferences but no plan; I had hopes but no models. I stood before the Lord, and my leadership team, with a blank piece of paper.

I needed the Mighty Mouse effect—a team of people who could save the day.

I **selected** four friends to work with me on this team. Most were people with whom I had a previous chemistry of friendship and mutual respect. Only one had an official organizational title; the remaining team members were field staff or part-time staff. In Navigators terms, they were everyday leaders within our organization.

Jake was a leader with experience gained from spending most of his career in the business world. Michael was a talented young leader who asked good questions and understood his generation. Pam was an insightful and skilled teacher who brought the priority of relationships to our mix. Janet brought her editing gifts and the ability to turn big tasks into practical action steps.

Our **pause** was the challenge I gave to the team: "Please pray about whether the Lord wants you to be involved." I outlined to each person the commitment of time and energy that would be needed. God came through; they all responded yes to my invitation.

Distance prohibited face-to-face meetings so we initially met through Zoom chats. We discussed our individual contributions to the team and developed a philosophy of training that would guide our discussion. This philosophy helped us **focus**.

After three or four months of Zoom meetings, we came together at my home for a two-day retreat. As we talked, enjoyed meals together, and prayed, the focus became clearer. We needed to create a training process that staff members could accomplish at their own pace without leaving home to attend a training session. Since nearly half our staff were bivocational, they didn't have the time or the resources to travel for expensive training sessions.

One key principle of our strategy was that training traveled in the vehicle of relationships: Staff members would not do this alone but would be paired with a trainer to help set goals and provide accountability and affirmation.

At the retreat, we **explored** a number of alternatives and ministry forms, filling page after page of large writing paper with our ideas. But the breakthrough came in a dinner discussion. Michael's concern was about the younger staff currently serving with us, as well as those we would recruit to our ministry.

"When they first encounter NCM," he observed, "they must feel that they're walking into a culture similar to their culture. I suggest we place our training on an interactive website and employ the advantages of social media."

This insight moved our thinking from traditional training approaches to a model that was still being developed in the business world. This social-media model would be driven by the principles of our training philosophy rather than by simply choosing a novel and contemporary approach.

Now the **plan** could be developed; work could be distributed according to our strengths. Jake became our liaison with the organization and our chief bargainer with website designers. Pam was the natural trainer and teacher who ensured the quality of our outcomes and kept us relationally focused. Janet was our editor, polishing the grammar and details of our documents. Michael gave helpful analysis and worked directly with the website designers to ensure that our plans were accomplished.

What was my role? I was the conductor, keeping the flow of the symphony going, allowing the team to play their individual parts, and guiding this orchestra to a crescendo of implementation.

We developed a timetable and action steps. We set a date to

launch our completed website, we developed a plan to help our staff become familiar with the new site, and we created a series of fun incentives for participation.

Where was our national leadership in this process? We developed our focus in consultation with them, but they released us to develop the plan. They didn't micromanage, hovering over us to make sure we did what was correct. They trusted us, gave us authority with responsibility, and released us.

At the time of this writing, more than half our staff members have been trained through our website, and the principles are being copied in other organizational settings. The influence of this training approach has gone international not only in training staff but also in modeling what staff training could look like.

One solitary leader—me—could not have accomplished this task. I knew virtually nothing about developing a website, working with web designers, preparing the training materials, and editing nearly a hundred pages of Bible studies and training exercises. I could lead the orchestra, though. By working together, we filled in a blank piece of paper with a training strategy and believed that God would create something out of nothing.

The Way of Cultural Wisdom

Everyday leaders need cultural wisdom to connect and influence their contexts.

Culture eats strategy for breakfast every time.

ATTRIBUTED TO PETER DRUCKER

DINNER AT THE MOWRY HOME is a time for Peggy and me to catch up on our days. It was during a dinner conversation that Peggy jolted me with these words: "I'm going to resign my teaching position and find a job in a corporate setting. I want to live as a light among unbelievers rather than stay in the safety of a Christian school."

I was surprised. I knew how much Peggy enjoyed teaching in a Christian school. She loved the relationships with her fellow teachers and the children, as well as the freedom to speak and teach from a biblical point of view. At the same time, I was thrilled that she wanted to take a radical step of obedience and live out her mission in a fresh way, leaving a Christian culture of comfort and familiarity to work in an unfamiliar culture.

I also saw an upside to this decision: Working in a corporate setting would pay more than teaching at a private Christian school! No matter the motive, neither of us, particularly Peggy, realized the challenges that lay ahead.

Peggy entered a completely different culture when she walked through the doors of the corporate office building on a bright Monday morning. What did she find behind those doors? She faced competition instead of camaraderie. Office memos replaced personal communication. A supervisor's demands for productivity replaced a principal's shepherding nature. Conversations were sprinkled with expletives instead of spiritual encouragement.

Peggy hadn't realized how easily she swam in a Christian culture until she was immersed in a high-octane corporate world. She was now swimming in a new pond. Moving to a new culture didn't require relocating to another country, learning a foreign language, or relating to unfamiliar people. Peggy merely drove to a different part of the city, met a new group of people, and did a different job.

This simple act put her in a new context, a new culture. Peggy needed to be a culture detective to spot the clues necessary to work, live, and succeed in this new culture. These clues would give her the cultural wisdom necessary to relate, contribute, and influence.

Everyday leaders live and lead in a variety of cultures. Most leaders choose to invest in one culture or context to live, work, or minister. No matter how large or small the culture is, it is challenging and changing. Understanding a culture empowers us to wisely bring people together to break new ground.

Describing "Culture"

When the word *culture* is mentioned, a variety of images may come to mind. For some people, their first thought is of the culture they

inherited from their ethnic or national background, which is typically a positive association. For a few, it's descriptive of someone
who has a wide range of experiences (i.e., a *cultured* person). Some
people view culture as a threat, referring to the secular environment that exists outside the church—"It's easy to be conformed to
our culture rather than to Jesus."

Trying to define *culture* is like taking a drink from a fire hose;
we're blown away by the complexity and enormity of the task. In
Perspectives on the World Christian Movement, missiologist Charles
Kraft defines *culture* as

> the label anthropologists give to the structured customs
> and underlying worldview assumptions [by] which people
> govern their lives. Culture . . . is a people's way of life,
> their design for living. . . . It consists of learned, patterned
> assumptions (worldview), concepts and behavior, plus
> the resulting artifacts (material culture).[1]

Coach and author Tina Stoltzfus Horst writes that "culture is the
distinctive characteristics—including values, attitudes, beliefs, and
behaviors—shared by a group (region, nation, people group, social
group, or organization)."[2] She pictures culture as an iceberg with the
largest portion submerged beneath the ocean's surface. The visible
part of the iceberg represents the behaviors of a culture, while the vast
part underneath the surface reflects the values and beliefs of a culture.[3]

Everyday leaders like me prefer a smaller drink of water. Here's
my simple definition:

> *A culture is a group of people who share a common language,*
> *values, story, and practices.*

Culture can be what I call a *macroculture*—the "big" culture of a nation (a French culture), an ethnic group (African American culture), or a regional area (southern culture). Some would call this a "dominant" culture—the cultural reality where one ethnicity or race sets the norms for others.

It is within these macrocultures that most of us swim daily. We're so used to this culture that we don't notice how familiar it is until we leave it. This happens every time we visit another country or venture into an ethnic enclave different from our own. This is the type of culture in which missionaries place themselves and learn how to minister cross-culturally.

Everyday leaders mostly live, lead, and minister in *microcultures*—workplaces, neighborhoods, churches, or families. The definition is still the same—"a group of people who share a common language, values, story, and practices"—but microcultures can be as small as a family or the company where we work.

Without an understanding of our particular cultures, we will fail to bring people together to break new ground. Understanding our cultures happens as everyday leaders grow in cultural wisdom by practicing the art of being culture detectives.

Weaving Together Culture and Wisdom

Culture is the local context where everyday leaders live and lead. What happens when we fail to understand our context—if we lack cultural wisdom? Let's return to the story of Peggy and her new job.

Peggy would suffer some consequences if she didn't understand, adjust to, and connect with the new culture of the corporate world. She needed cultural wisdom. This meant learning how to navigate in a working culture of diverse ages and lifestyles, the language of new IT systems, and the unwritten codes of advancement and relationships.

Cultural wisdom is more than cultural awarenesss or sensitivity. It's this and more. Cultural wisdom gives us the ability to wisely relate to, understand, and adapt to culturally diverse situations and a variety of people. We understand within this particular cultural context how to apply God's standards for what is good and right—how to nourish and give life to people, as well as how to be fair and just in relationships and work practices. Cultural wisdom is applying God's wisdom to a particular context in order to live and influence for the Kingdom.

Two examples point the way to cultural wisdom's value: farming and preaching. Both require lifelong learning.

Let's talk about farming. Novelist and agrarian philosopher Wendell Berry writes that good farmers "consult the genius of the place." By "genius" he means the prevalent quality of a culture or place. Farmers become students of their land in order to "ask what nature would permit them to do there, and what they could do there with the least harm to the place and to their natural and human neighbors."[4]

Farmers' knowledge of their land enables them to "tend farms that they know and love . . . using tools and methods that they know and love."[5] Since the farmer knows and loves their place, intelligent farmers "who desire the long-term success of farming . . . adapt their work to their places"; this means "fit[ting] the farming to the land."[6] Out of love, the farmer wisely adapts tools, methods, and expectations to the land they farm.

Farmers have learned that it's difficult to grow pineapples in Vermont or bananas in Alaska. Studying the genius of the place—the context—yields the cultural wisdom needed to determine what will grow.

We may not be farmers, but we can learn from their example. Everyday leaders need cultural wisdom to effectively live and minister in the context or cultures we're placed in. This wisdom enables us to adapt to the place, use the appropriate tools, discover our limitations, and have realistic expectations. Farmers need to be learners to farm well; the same goes for leaders who want to lead well. Now let's examine preaching.

I sat in my seat attentively listening to Pastor Nate's presentation on how to teach and preach to millennials. His opening statement caught my attention: "Our church chooses to look at our audience through the lens of Acts 17, not Acts 2." My curiosity was immediately aroused. What did he mean by this?

Acts 17 includes Paul's sermon to a pagan Athenian audience. In Acts 2, Peter preaches to a Jewish audience. The starting points, arguments, and language differ widely between the two audiences.

Peter appealed to his listeners by citing a familiar prophecy from the Hebrew prophet Joel (Acts 2:16-21). He then built a case using Old Testament examples and references (2:29-31) to establish Jesus as "both Lord and Messiah" (2:36). Peter had the cultural wisdom to appeal to shared language, values, stories, and practices of the Jewish people to build a persuasive argument.

In today's setting, this audience would be people who grew up in a church culture—they're familiar with and sympathetic to "church" language, Christian values, Bible stories, and worship practices. What happens if the audience changes?

Paul's Athenian audience in Acts 17 had zero or very limited knowledge of Jewish history and its sacred writings. His starting point was an altar to an "unknown god" (Acts 17:23), not a mention of a prophet. His references were Greek poets (17:28), not the Old Testament writers. He appealed to God's general revelation (17:24-27), not to the Old Testament Scriptures. His cultural wisdom led him to appeal to the language, values, stories, and practices of a people very different from a Jewish audience.

Scholar Richard Longenecker wrote that it "would be futile [for Paul] to refer to a history no one knew or argue from fulfillment of prophecy no one was interested in or quote from a book no one read or accepted as authoritative. . . . Instead he took [as] his point of contact . . . an altar he had seen in the city."[7]

Missiologist Charles Kraft calls this the principle of being "receptor oriented."[8] This means communicating in ways that can be received or understood by the hearer. To become receiver oriented, we collect clues about our context from the words, objects, or stories that appear in the hearer's culture in order to meet people where they are. We follow in God's preferred means of communication: "He uses the language and thought patterns of those to whom He speaks. . . . [He seeks] to *adapt* to us, to enter our frame of reference" in order to communicate.[9] Cultural wisdom enables us to follow in the pattern of our Lord to wisely connect our message to its listeners.

Pastor Nate sees today's audience as more like the Athenians in Acts 17 than the Jews in Acts 2. Many people in today's culture have little or no Christian background, almost no understanding of the Christian "language" or values, little understanding of the gospel story, and no practice of the Christian faith. Cultural wisdom is needed to connect with this group of people. This wisdom begins with the discipline of being a lifelong learner.

Let's personalize this by returning to Peggy's experience. She had to learn the language of her new workplace: both the technical language of the business and also the social language of everyday conversations. While many businesses post their corporate values in a handbook, there are other implied workplace values to be discovered. These could include: What dress is appropriate? Are we expected to work overtime if needed to complete a project? What are the unwritten expectations to get noticed for advancement? The corporate story is prominent in some businesses and can include the history of the founder or a biography of the current CEO.

Finally, Peggy had to learn the practices of the workplace, practices that were both explicit (formal training) and implicit (informal learning)—such as how to network with coworkers for technical support or discerning the unwritten codes for relating to her coworkers.

Collecting clues in these areas would give Peggy insight into the shared life of people in her work setting. Gaining cultural wisdom means drawing upon these insights to help you choose the good and the right way to live and work. The character of God, found in his wisdom, is the grid through which we assess and live out the values we discover in a culture.

To stay true to her sense of calling to the corporate world, Peggy needed cultural wisdom to influence this culture. She needed insight on how to start faith conversations or apply God's Kingdom values to this setting. Her immersion in this culture presented challenges to her faith. What does it mean to be "in the world" but not "of the world" (John 17:16, author's paraphrase)? How could she insulate herself from the world's influence without isolating herself from others (John 17:15-19)? Answering these questions requires a marriage between cultural wisdom and God's wisdom.

In summary, we need cultural wisdom so that:

- *We can connect and communicate.* Learning a culture's language and values enables us to communicate and relate to people within that culture. We learn the other's point of view, their language and values, so that we can communicate in ways that are understandable.

- *We can be enriched and developed.* Culture can be a teacher for life and work. Cultural wisdom helps us build relationships with coworkers who have the potential to enrich our lives as friends and help us succeed in our tasks.

- *We can influence while guarding against being influenced.* Cultural wisdom enables us to build bridges of trust and communication, the essentials for influence. God's wisdom helps us choose what is biblically good and right when our values conflict with cultural values.

Cultural wisdom is the fruit of being a culture detective. Culture detectives spot clues, ask questions, and form deductions about cultures in order to grow in and practice cultural wisdom.

We Need to Be like Sherlock Holmes

Sherlock Holmes is the gold standard for detectives. When we hear his name, multiple images flood our minds—the pipe, the cloak and cap, the violin, and the hawk-like profile. The nineteenth-century mastermind of 221B Baker Street, London, inhabits every generation of crime stories and detectives.

We're fascinated by this iconic figure who wisely observes, questions, and deduces in order to solve the most perplexing crimes. Every detective in every movie or television series follows in the footsteps of Sherlock Holmes. In fact, Holmes holds the Guinness World Record for the "most portrayed literary human character in film and TV."[10]

However, what he offers us is more than a way to solve crimes. Author Maria Konnikova describes Holmes's example as "an entire way of thinking, a mindset that can be applied to countless enterprises far removed from the foggy streets of the London underworld. It is an approach . . . [that] can serve as a model for thinking, a way of being, even, just as powerful in our time as it was in Conan Doyle's."[11] We want to adopt this mindset—this "way of being"— to understand culture, the context in which we live and lead.

Holmes is an ideal model for how to collect clues through observation and questions in order to form deductions or reach conclusions about a puzzling crime. The puzzle for us is understanding the culture in which we live and lead, not to solve a crime. Everyday leaders aren't out to capture criminals but to capture the wisdom needed to create everyday strategies for everyday challenges. This wisdom is captured as we "detect" or notice things that others often overlook—what the dictionary calls the "very slight."

Like Sherlock Holmes, culture detectives need to know how to make observations, ask questions, and form deductions that need to be tested. But first, since character trumps competency, we must examine ourselves to ensure we have the required character.

The Character of a Culture Detective

The Practice of Humility

My disciple-making ministry lands me in a diversity of denominations. I work with Lutheran churches and Assemblies of God, Methodist and Southern Baptist churches, Nazarene churches and

Vineyard churches. Each denomination and local church has a culture that I need to be sensitive to. Pastor Ryan graciously informed me of this during one of our first phone calls.

We talked through his commitment and my commitment to the culture-building process. Then as our conversation was coming to an end, Ryan made a pointed comment.

"We recently finished a contractual arrangement with a fundraising organization," he said. "I respected this organization, but I did give them this piece of advice: 'You're an expert on fundraising, but I'm an expert on my congregation.'"

There was a delicate pause after this statement. It hung in the air not as a threat but as a veiled caution from Ryan to me. I may be an expert on disciplemaking, but he was an expert on his congregation.

Ryan understood his people. He knew their likes and dislikes, what would work and wouldn't work. Ryan knew people's stories because he entered their hurts and hopes on a daily basis. He knew his church's culture; he understood the context.

The veiled challenge to me was that I must be careful not to presume that I automatically knew what was best for Ryan's church. I needed to proceed with a spirit of humility.

Humility should be the dye that colors all our relationships, particularly as we enter into cultures different from our own. The apostle Paul gives us this exhortation: "In humility count others more significant than yourselves" (Philippians 2:3, ESV). The apostle Peter extends the theme of humility, asking us to maintain a "humble mind," not repaying evil for evil, but choosing to bless (1 Peter 3:8-9, ESV).

Humility affects how we understand our workplaces, neighborhoods, or church cultures. Tina Stoltzfus Horst writes that "humility is defined as modesty and respect, not behaving as though you are more important than the other. Humility . . . means being willing to enter the cross-cultural relationship as a learner who must acquire the basics."[12] This means learning from others about what works in their culture, what values are important to them, and what pace and elements of leadership will serve them best.

Nobody likes a know-it-all; rather, people appreciate a leader who's considerate of their feelings and context. Character trumps competency, and humility is a mark of character that's critical for culture detectives.

The Practice of Respect

Walking into a church service different from my own is like walking into another culture. I'm of the Baptist persuasion, so I like my services simple. In our typical worship services, we have some announcements, a couple of contemporary songs, one or two public prayers, and then a thirty-minute message. We're also governed by a set of implied, and sometimes explicit, baptistic values of order, limited emotionalism, and informality.

This is the Sunday routine I'm used to. Imagine the culture shock of walking into a Lutheran service.

Lutherans have a formal order to worship that leads people from confession to forgiveness to praise to teaching to mission. I found myself echoing the liturgical readings to the pastor. Then we stopped in the middle of the service to do something called "pass the peace." I also went forward and knelt to receive Communion rather than it being served to me. And the message was Bible based but lasted around fifteen minutes.

I had to choose my attitude—would I critique this service as inferior to what I was used to, or would I respect it and choose to learn more about it? I chose the route of respect.

I respected the service by taking the time to understand it. There's a story and meaning behind each step of worship, and I was touched as I learned more. It was different from my typical Baptist experience, but I chose to respect and understand rather than judge.

The New Testament teaches that every relationship we have should be marked by respect. Respect happens in the political arena (Romans 13:5-7), in marriage (Ephesians 5:33), with those outside the faith (1 Thessalonians 4:12), and in work relationships (Ephesians 6:5). Our church leaders should be "worthy of respect" (1 Timothy 3:8). Just in case we missed someone, the apostle Peter exhorts us to "show proper respect to everyone" (1 Peter 2:17). In other words, respect is foundational to every human and societal relationship.

Respect fundamentally means admiring the character or achievements of others. It also conveys a consideration of their feelings and rights. Honor and respect are closely tied together (see Romans 12:10). We honor people by giving credit to their accomplishments. When we respect their culture, we give credit, honor, and esteem to their language, values, story, and practices.

When we enter another culture different from our own— a workplace, church, neighborhood, or even a family—we must show respect. Here are some simple acts of respect we can cultivate:

- Educating ourselves beforehand about a different culture and its values
- Having a posture of learning and asking questions when necessary

- Affirming what we see and experience
- Enjoying rather than critiquing the culture
- Gaining an appreciation for the culture and sharing your experience with others

Respect is commanded to be given but not pursued. We're to "outdo one another in showing honor" (Romans 12:10, ESV). We run to give honor rather than working to receive honor. When we fail to respect a culture, we fail in understanding, we lose an opportunity to influence, and we walk away poorer because of our judgmental spirit.

The Practice of Curiosity

My Navigator career has planted me in a variety of life and professional contexts. One of my most unusual ministry settings was the medical community—physicians and dentists. The medical community is a culture with a common language, values, story, and practices different from other professions.

What does this culture look like? It's a very hierarchical culture. Pediatricians and family practitioners reside near the bottom of the esteem pyramid, while specialized surgeons occupy the upper echelons. Support staff rule the profession, controlling the scheduling, finances, and access to the doctors. There's both a generalized language for physicians and a more specialized language for specialists. They all share the same hazing-experience story—the rigors of residency—and this experience is an unspoken bond.

I walked into this setting with a certain naivete. I thought doctors and dentists were like any businesspeople. What saved me from a disastrous experience was the humility of curiosity. Instead of presuming to know about the life of a physician or dentist, I decided to ask questions—a lot of questions.

When you ask questions, you respect people. Questions communicate that who they are, what they do, or how they spend their days is important. It's so important that you're choosing to take the time to find out about it. Questions demonstrate a humble spirit.

In asking questions, I practiced curiosity. According to the *Oxford Dictionary of English*, *curiosity* simply means "a strong desire to know or learn something."[13] It can range from something as mundane as finding out how to unplug a blocked sink (a skill I learned from YouTube) or as spiritual as wading through Calvin's *Institutes* (I was curious to see what he taught rather than depending on the interpretation of others). I believe that Jesus uses our natural curiosity to point the way to his Kingdom.

It should be no surprise that Jesus deliberately shifted the traditional narrative about God, people, and faith. The surprise is that he did this through curiosity—asking question after question of rich and poor, religious and irreligious, men and women. Author Casey Tygrett writes that "the point of Jesus' questions was to stoke curiosity rather than seeing it as an obstacle or a problem. . . . He invited people to explore and think along with him."[14]

Jesus' questions make me curious about the Kingdom, who my neighbor is, and what the greatest commandment is. Jesus didn't ask questions to satisfy his own curiosity or to gain information. He asked questions to arouse curiosity that engaged people in thinking, reflecting, and relating to others.

Let's be honest: The older we become, the fewer questions we ask. I think it's because we're afraid to communicate that we don't know something. If I lack knowledge, I must be weak. When we ask questions we become unguarded, demonstrating a certain fragility or vulnerability. Curiosity is one mark of humility.

Three Skills for Culture Detectives

What skills do we need to become culture detectives? What will help us grow in cultural wisdom? Three skills are primary.

Skill No. 1: Make Observations

A group of us walked through the jammed office space of cubicles and people to our conference meeting room. Along the way, we couldn't help but observe the actions of the staff.

"Do you know what I noticed?" said one of our group, a successful entrepreneur who had started several businesses. "Nobody seems to be in a hurry. A lot of conversations are taking place between workspaces. Phones are ringing, and no one rushes to answer. People are casually walking around without any apparent purpose. I wonder what kind of culture is being created."

In just a few minutes, my friend had made several key observations. He could do this because he had trained himself to notice what takes place in successful offices. He had the skilled eye of one who was trained in making observations.

Detectives of crime and culture are skilled observers. Criminal detectives are looking for clues to identify a perpetrator. Culture detectives are looking for clues about a culture, observations that give insights into a context. To become astute culture detectives, we must learn to observe.

Our model Sherlock Holmes was famous for his observational skills. His "seemingly superhuman ability to deduce a series of accurate facts from seemingly insignificant clues [was] something akin to magic." But this ability isn't magic, writes Greg McKeown. "It is the difference between seeing and observing, between watching and noticing."[15]

Observation requires diligent and focused attention to the subject at hand. We must learn to practice mindfulness, not mindlessness. Seeing is an automatic experience for us. We seldom think about what we see. Our eyes are bombarded daily with an array of images. Mindlessness unthinkingly absorbs this sensory overload. We become passive observers, never processing what we see.

Familiarity leads to mindlessness. For years I rode the city bus down High Street in Columbus, Ohio, to my campus ministry at The Ohio State University. The route had become so familiar that I no longer noticed my surroundings as I sat at my window seat. A big-box store could've been built at one of the major intersections, and I never would have noticed it! I had stopped looking. No wonder Jesus equated spiritual obstinacy with blindness.

The nativity narrative in Matthew's Gospel speaks to what it means to truly observe. The magi from the east saw the Messiah's star and went looking for the King to worship (Matthew 2:1-12). They came to Jerusalem, expecting the Jews to know the location of the Messiah's birth. The Jewish religious leaders knew the location—"in Bethlehem in Judea" (2:5)—but they missed the star. They weren't looking. They were so familiar with the prophecies that they stopped watching and expecting.

But some pagan wise men looked and found the Messiah. They came to worship him, but many of the religious leaders missed the moment—"Though seeing, they do not see" (Matthew 13:13). Familiarity can lead to blindness; we fail to see because we have stopped paying attention.

We must train our minds to focus, to pay attention, to be mindful. This follows the Sherlock Holmes principle: "How much an observant man might learn by an accurate and systematic examination of all that came his way."[16] Mindfulness is fixing our attention on the present, "ignoring all the noise in our environment" to focus on the now.[17]

Skilled observers not only focus on observing a few things at a time; they are intentional about what they observe. This means looking in a mindful, present fashion that fixates on the moment, choosing what to observe rather than going with the flow. This discipline is acquired through practice.

Here's a sampling of the things culture detectives can focus their attention on when observing the culture of a workplace, neighborhood, or family:

- What kinds of clothes do people wear?
- What makes people laugh?
- What makes people angry or disappointed?
- What media do they watch?
- How are they considerate toward children?
- What are people talking about or reading?

Culture detectives are not mind*less*—casting their attention on any passing moment. They are mind*ful*—disciplining their attention to focus on select things. They make choices about what to look at rather than engaging in haphazard sensory overkill.

Skill No. 2: Ask Questions

When the "sold" sign came down on the house next door, Peggy and I were eager to meet our new neighbors. It took a couple of weeks, but we finally coordinated our schedules to have Steve and Linda over for dessert.

What happens when you meet someone new? You immediately begin asking questions to collect information about each other. Discovering basic facts about another person's life establishes some common ground upon which to build a friendship. Here's how the information-gathering process went for Steve and me.

"Where did you grow up?" I asked Steve.

"In Clyde, Ohio," he said.

"I know Clyde. I used to drive through it when I went to college" was my reply.

"So did you grow up near Clyde?" asked Steve.

"Milan," I replied.

"Really?" said Steve. "One of my best friends in high school was from Milan."

"No kidding," I said. "Who was he?"

"His name was Dennis James," replied Steve.

"You're kidding! Dennis was one of my best high school friends."

"Dennis and I were in a rock band together during high school. I was the rhythm guitarist," said Steve.

"Really? I used to travel with Dennis's band. I even went with the band during a recording session."

We quickly deduced that we had met each other nearly thirty years ago as teenagers who shared a common friend. This is what's meant by a "small world."

We reached our conclusion by asking each other questions. We collected enough clues that led us to a common conclusion: We both loved rock and roll and had a common friend named Dennis. Questions are a culture detective's best friend.

Questions dominate the Bible. A question marked the first

recorded exchange between the Creator and Adam (Genesis 3:9). Jesus understood the power of a good question and asked a lot of them. We notice that his questions were simple, clear, never condescending, always provocative. They were attuned to the unique needs of the people he was talking to.

In describing our model detective Sherlock Holmes, Maria Konnikova writes, "One of the things that characterizes Holmes's thinking . . . is a natural skepticism and inquisitiveness toward the world. Nothing is taken at face value. Everything is scrutinized and considered."[18] He was always asking questions, always looking for clues, always being curious.

One of my first steps in ministering to churches is to visit the church and the staff. I want to observe people in their natural habitat to understand the context of their ministry and the church. As we tour the facilities, I ask a lot of questions. Here's a sample:

- When was the church built?
- What were the original members like?
- What's descriptive about your neighborhood?
- What do you enjoy about this building?
- Are there any changes you would like to make?
- What is a worship service like in your church now?
- How has this changed over the years?
- What are characteristics of a typical attendee at your church?
- How has the typical attendee changed over the years?

I'm naturally curious about the church. I want to collect clues about the culture that give me insight into the story, values, and vision of the church.

A simple illustration helps guide my question asking. I call it the "question-asking triangle."[19] *Trust* forms the base of the triangle. We can't ask questions that are personal or deep without trust. Trust also creates a setting for honesty and transparency.

In her book *How to Ask Great Questions*, Karen Lee-Thorp writes that an "environment . . . in which people feel welcomed . . . is the kind most likely to encourage people to consider new ideas, examine their lives, and entertain the possibility of changing their behavior."[20] Trust creates openness and responsiveness to questions.

The second side of the question-asking triangle is *timing*. We all know how powerful a good question can be when asked at just the right time. We're also painfully aware of the effects of a poorly timed question. Asking the right questions at the right time requires trusting the Holy Spirit to guide us.

The third side of the triangle is *type*. There are many types of questions we can ask. Some questions clarify, others analyze, some provoke debate, and a select few cause people to imagine.

Culture detectives need a toolbox full of different types of questions. We have six tools in our toolbox that can help us skillfully ask good questions. These tools are: who, what, where, when, why, and how. Take a moment to review the questions I listed earlier that I typically ask when I visit churches. Notice the variety of ways I employ these six questions as I relate to leaders.

While criminal detectives may interrogate people, culture

detectives exhibit humble curiosity by asking questions. Because we respect a person's culture or context, we're curious to learn more about it. We ask questions not to pass judgment or to catch people in a mental slipup but to understand and appreciate their culture. Culture detectives are collecting clues to gain wisdom about a culture in order to be relevant, enriched, and influential. This means asking questions.

Skill No. 3: Make Deductions

Peggy and I moved to Columbus, Ohio, from a small college located in a rural community. We began "church shopping" soon after we settled into our new home. The first church we visited reminded us of the style of worship, language, and preaching in our former church. During our second visit, we attended an adult Sunday school class. When we broke up into small groups, I made a quick observation and soon became embarrassed.

As I looked around the circle, I noticed that our clothes were out-of-date. I deduced that we would need to change our wardrobe to come to this church! We obviously didn't share the professional look of the people around us. Now, this wasn't a wealthy church; it's just that people dressed more fashionably than in our previous rural community.

My observation about what people wore led me to conclude that we needed some new clothes (and increase our clothing budget!). This slightly humorous situation showed me what it meant to be a culture detective.

"Deduction," writes Konnikova, is "the moment when you put together all of the elements . . . in a single, cohesive whole that makes sense of the full picture."[21]

We can compare the deductive process to a funnel. At the wide end of the funnel, we're collecting clues through observation and questions, accumulating a wealth of information about a culture. Now it's time to narrow our findings and wisely form some conclusions. However, before jumping to conclusions, it's helpful to take a simple pause and ask some personal questions.

We all have a mental and emotional grid through which we filter information and make deductions. While our aim is to create a biblical grid, to think as Jesus thinks, the reality is that we sometimes allow our assumptions and preferences to construct this grid. This is commonly referred to as an "unconscious bias." Unconsciously, we have a particular bias toward people, values, and beliefs that color the deductions we make.

When Peggy entered the workforce of the corporate world, she was one of the older people on the team. Her supervisor was a younger man. Peggy unconsciously equated age with maturity and wisdom. While this may be true some of the time, it's not a universal truth. People younger than us can have maturity and wisdom. Peggy chose to put aside her bias and give her supervisor a chance. He proved to be a capable leader who valued Peggy's contribution. If she had clung to her bias about age, the relationship would have been hampered. Cultural wisdom saved the day.

We must ask ourselves two honest questions to reveal our biases:

1. Do I have any preconceived ideas about people (gender, ethnicity, race, religion, age) that could color my conclusions?

2. Do I have any strong opinions and preferences about how ministry should be done or where it happens?

Besides our bias in forming conclusions, another element to be cautious of is forming hasty deductions. We can quickly deduce something that might be culturally inaccurate or insensitive. To prevent this, we need what my friend Stowe calls "honesty brokers." Honesty brokers are insiders to the culture, members of the community. They are people we trust and who trust us. We can honestly share our observations with them and solicit their critique. As insiders, they help us decide whether our deductions are accurate.

Finally, we must filter our deductions through our biblical grids. These grids are the two wisdom paths of fixed commands and principled thinking. Not everything we observe and deduce about a culture may be ethical or just. The reality is that cultures are part of the world system—"the powers of this dark world and . . . the spiritual forces of evil in the heavenly realms" (Ephesians 6:12). The Scriptures provide the light necessary to do the good and the right—the wise thing—in our cultural settings (Psalm 119:105).

Everyday leaders will grow in cultural wisdom as they practice these three basic skills of being a culture detective. This cultural wisdom will help us relate, lead, and contribute in ways that are biblically good and right, nourishing people and settings, leading with justice and fairness.

The Culture Detective's Investigative Grid

Our model detective, Sherlock Holmes, didn't simply look at and ask about anything that came into his range of vision or curiosity. Like Holmes, we must think in a "mindful, present fashion, to exert effort on what goes through our heads instead of going with the flow."[22] He was a disciplined and intentional detective. We must learn from his intentionality and practice using an investigative grid.

The following grid will provide you with a disciplined direction to investigate the culture around you. I call it the Culture Detective's Investigative Grid. The grid is built around our simple definition of *culture*: A culture is a group of people who share a common language, values, story, and practices. Within each quadrant of this grid are two simple questions that you can use to get started.

LANGUAGE	VALUES
What are some common words?	*What do people love?*
What words are unique to this context?	*What are their interests?*
STORY	PRACTICES
What is the "origin" story?	*What is expected?*
What is the personal story?	*What is rewarded?*

Language. The first quadrant is language. Language is an important clue to detect and collect. Suppose you're ministering to a postmillennial culture. What are some common words this age group uses? Are there words unique to this group of people? Looking at the language used in Spotify, TikTok, or Instagram is a great place to start making observations about words.

Values. A second clue-rich source is values. What can you observe about what postmillennials love? What is their favorite music, fashion, celebrities, media personalities, and food? What are their interests and their points of concern? You might discover an interest in environmental or social justice issues. These points of interest may be very different from those of an older population.

Story. The third quadrant is story. Author and musician Sho Baraka writes, "Stories have the ability to cultivate societies. Or to kill them. . . . Every group is fashioned by a story."[23] In the story are heroes and villains. There's an origin story, a point of beginning for a culture. For example, if you're collecting clues about The Navigators, you would discover our origin story in the ministry of founder Dawson Trotman.

Besides the origin story, there's the importance of the personal story. A personal story sets the context for the individual. "You see, we live the story we believe," notes Baraka.[24] For example, you might ask why someone moved to a particular neighborhood or accepted a certain job. Knowing this personal story would give you clues about their values and goals and how they shape the story they're living.

Practices. In the fourth quadrant, we collect clues about shared practices. In a workplace culture, outside of job performance, what behaviors are expected? For example: What are the boundaries for relating to those of the opposite sex? What is considered humorous, and what is offensive? What dress standards are stated (perhaps in the HR manual), and which ones are implied? It's important to remember that not all practices may be appropriate for a believer. We need wisdom to choose what is good and right to God.

THE WAY OF CULTURAL WISDOM

We often behave in a certain way because it will be rewarded. What practices are rewarded in a workplace—practices that might not show up in one's job performance review but are culturally present in hidden ways? For example, working overtime is not required, but there's a subtle expectation from the employer that working overtime shows loyalty. It will be noticed and rewarded even though it's not in one's job description.

We need cultural wisdom to wisely bring people together to break new ground. Cultural wisdom allows us to do what is good and right in the context that the Lord has placed us in.

Your First Detective Assignment

1. Identify the culture you need to collect clues about. It could be a youth ministry, a neighborhood, a workplace, a church, a volunteer association, or an ethnic group.

2. Develop a simple plan to employ the Culture Detective's Investigative Grid.

3. Identify some honesty brokers—cultural insiders who will affirm, clarify, or correct your conclusions.

4. Make some deductions or conclusions about what you've observed.

5. Either individually or with a group of people, discuss the implications of your observations. How can ministry or service be impacted by an understanding of the culture?

In the appendix is a training exercise for cultural wisdom. Consider using it within your current neighborhood, workplace, or ministry culture. You can engage others in this exercise by identifying a culture that a few of you share. As a group, walk through the exercise.

A Case Study in Cultural Wisdom

Stan and Denise are everyday leaders, serving as the pastoral staff in an urban-poor setting. Their neighborhood is populated by people who moved from rural Appalachia to work in the urban factories in the 1960s and 1970s. The culture of Appalachia and generational poverty have shaped this neighborhood. Denise and Stan need cultural wisdom; they must become culture detectives.

Both of these everyday leaders came from suburban churches. When they began their ministry, they admitted to having some "bias" about poverty and what successful ministry should look like. They soon found that many of the ministry methods and resources used in their former suburban experience weren't relevant to this particular culture.

Stan and Denise began making **observations** about their neighborhood. To their surprise, they observed that relationships weren't built inside the home but on front porches, front yards, or sidewalks. People always seemed to be outside and were more available than in suburban neighborhoods.

They also discovered many homes led by single moms or with multiple generations living together, such as grandparents living with their grandchildren. Home life was complicated by the intersections of multiple relationships, inconsistent employment, and dysfunctions amplified through poverty.

Stan noted a major break with suburban culture when it came to the transparency of the people. "Probably 60 percent of our congregation has gone through or is in a recovery program," he said. "We don't wear any masks in our worship or our relationships! People are so honest about their lives and have a hunger to change. This is so refreshing compared to suburban settings."

Another observation was the obvious poverty of the neighborhood. High rent prices drove generations to live together. Food poverty was present, so food banks were the lifeblood of many people. Basic resources like counseling, money management, or medical care were limited. Many people were in transition between jobs or were transitioning from incarceration.

These men and women were interested in the same things people in every neighborhood desire: "How can we secure good employment?" "How can we plan a better future for our children?" "How do we care for the well-being of our neighborhoods?" "What can we do to improve our schools?"

Stan and Denise decided to see their observations not as disadvantages but as advantages. They loved the friendliness of people, the availability of people's schedules, and the honesty of people's lives. When the gospel took root in a person's life, there was real change—and everyone would soon hear about it!

The need for relevant and practical small groups emerged as a critical need for the growth of their church. But there were some challenges.

Communal life happened outside the home. Living situations were often crowded and inconsistent, with people coming in and out of the home and in and out of employment. Meeting in restaurants or coffee shops was ineffective. There were few restaurants in urban neighborhoods, and with limited discretionary income, people didn't gather in these public settings as they did in a suburban culture.

The bias in suburban cultures was toward house churches. Elaborate theologies were built around the house church movement. But they wondered what happened if this form didn't fit the culture.

Denise and Stan reached a simple but profound **deduction** about small group ministry. They knew that the *function* of people gathering together was important no matter the culture. But the *form* of meeting in a home didn't fit here. What did fit?

The answer was simple: People could meet in the church building.

Their church was already a neighborhood church. They didn't need more parking spaces, since people walked to church. The church was a place of safety and continuity. It was more likely that small groups could thrive in the church building rather than in someone's living room.

Stan and Denise could have allowed their suburban biases to color their conclusions but chose instead to surrender these preferences.

In suburbia, people are often encouraged to get out of the church and decentralize the building except for worship. This pastoral team has chosen to rise above their preferences and past experiences to affirm an old but still relevant ministry form: the church building.

They understand that the form must be relevant to the culture to be effective. They are growing in and applying cultural wisdom as they practice being culture detectives.

The Way of Innovation

Everyday leaders wisely create new and innovative strategies for local challenges.

The nature of a machine is to do the same thing over and over again so long as it keeps going.

DOROTHY SAYERS, *THE MIND OF THE MAKER*

MY FIRST COMPUTER was a hand-me-down NCR that a friend gave me. With only brief instructions, I tackled the task of composing my workshop notes on this strange machine. There were so many commands in this complex word processor that after two hours I quit and went back to my trusty typewriter!

I never sat in front of another personal computer until a friend introduced me to his Mac a year later. The simplicity of this computer hooked me for life.

I didn't realize that I was entering a Macintosh cult, with the supreme leader, Steve Jobs, directing his followers. I ultimately became acquainted with Jobs through Walter Isaacson's biography. Jobs understood innovation because he understood form and function.

Steve Jobs revolutionized the product-design industry by marrying aesthetics and function. In other words, could we have a beautifully designed product without sacrificing its purpose? A beautifully designed form (the appearance of a computer) should fit the computer's functions. This marriage of aesthetics and function transformed product design, a change we're still benefiting from today.

Modernism's goal of creating simple, clean products for the masses shaped Jobs's thinking. "He believed," wrote Isaacson, "that great industrial design—a colorfully simple logo, a sleek case for the Apple II—would set the company apart and make its products distinctive."[1] Again, he wanted to marry aesthetics with function.

Designing something beautiful meant keeping it simple. "'Simplicity is the ultimate sophistication,'" Jobs declared. Simplicity showed up in the Mac's design, but something else also drove Jobs's passion. "'The main thing in our design is that we have to make things intuitively obvious.'"[2] This meant using metaphors in the computer's functions, such as a desktop or a trash can, symbols that people can intuitively and quickly grasp.

"From his father," writes Isaacson, "Jobs had learned that a hallmark of passionate craftsmanship is making sure that even the aspects that will remain hidden are done beautifully." This led Jobs to scrutinize the computer's circuit board, taking something purely functional and designing it "'to be as beautiful as possible, even if it's inside the box.'"[3] Isaacson explains how the Apple team celebrated their innovative new product:

> When the design was finally locked in, Jobs called the
> Macintosh team together for a ceremony. "Real artists

sign their work," he said. So he got out a sheet of drafting paper and a Sharpie pen and had all of them sign their names. The signatures were engraved inside each Macintosh. No one would ever see them, but the members of the team knew that their signatures were inside, just as they knew that the circuit board was laid out as elegantly as possible. . . . "With moments like this, he got us seeing our work as art," said Atkinson [a design team member].[4]

Innovation is something beautiful, creative, and functional. Innovation is the breaking of *new* ground as we bring people together.

A Case for Innovation

Everyday leaders are growing in the realization that cookie-cutter solutions are no longer adequate. We enjoy buying off-the-shelf solutions because it's efficient and easy—little hard work is required. However, local challenges demand innovative local solutions. It takes work, but God has created us with an innovative nature that can be harnessed and released with the Holy Spirit's help. We need his wisdom to bring people together and break new ground.

I so appreciate Wendell Berry's insight when he quoted John Todd, who wrote that we must create "elegant solutions predicated on the uniqueness of [every] place."[5] Collaboration and cultural wisdom will give us the insight necessary for these "elegant solutions" crafted by local leaders for local challenges.

Unfortunately, most worship settings, evangelism strategies, and disciple-making ministries have a high familiarity with one another. In their book *The Shaping of Things to Come*, authors Michael Frost and Alan Hirsch write, "It sometimes seems as if there is some form of 'template' at work in evangelical churches all over the world, regardless of language and culture."[6]

I used to regularly travel to Eastern European countries to help pastors and churches develop disciple-making ministries. Imagine my surprise when I attended a worship service and knew all the songs we sang. The words were in a different language, but I recognized the tunes—we sang the same songs in my home church. In fact, if it wasn't for the language, the entire service could have been lifted from this location and planted in my home church, and no one would have known the difference.

It's easy to leave our creative God parked outside the doors of our ministries and churches. What could happen if we brought the mind of an artist or the imagination of an inventor to bear on leading a youth ministry, designing a worship service, or encouraging evangelism? What if we practiced the Great Commission in artful and innovative ways filled with faith, creativity, and risk?

Today's challenges—the fastballs of change—require new and inventive ministry forms for everyday leaders. The insights gained from lifelong learning, the wisdom from understanding our culture or context, and the collective imaginations of collaboration all serve to create that which doesn't exist: new and innovative strategies and approaches for life and ministry. Everyday leaders must harness their God-given imaginations to wisely innovate and create new strategies and resources—the breaking of new ground—that are good and right for each context.

I hope this chapter unlocks your creative and innovative side in Spirit-filled ways. In the words of author and philosopher Francis

Schaeffer: "The Christian is the one whose imagination should fly beyond the stars."[7]

A Brief Theology of Creativity

Let's make another trip to the Garden.

Human creativity is rooted in divine creativity. We create because God created first. God is introduced in Genesis as a creative artist. Before we know anything about him, we can observe his first acts. He created things and then pronounced them "good" (Genesis 1:31).

What can we discover about God's creative side? He could have created a dull world, a bland world, a world with a limited variety of insects. Instead, he created a world awash in color, a world flavored with taste and smell, a world inhabited by 925,000 different kinds of insects! Poet Scott Cairns calls him the "Mad Architect of exuberant abundance."[8] This is our creative God!

When we first read about the image of God in Genesis, we see one thing: The narrative shows us that God, the creator of the world, made humans "in his image" (1:27). Being in his image means that people, like God, are creators.

In her book *The Mind of the Maker*, author Dorothy Sayers expands on this creative act:

> In the passage leading up to the statement about man,
> [the author of Genesis] has given no detailed information
> about God. Looking at man, he sees in him something
> essentially divine, but when we turn back to see what he
> says about the original upon which the "image" of God

was modelled, we find only the single assertion, "God created." The characteristic common to God and man is apparently that: the desire and the ability to make things.[9]

It would be easy to think of God only as the great artist and innovator, or as the poet-painter William Blake portrayed him in his famous painting, *God as Architect*.[10] God is all these and much more.

It would also be inaccurate to describe creativity as simply creating something new or novel. "Novelty, simply as such," writes C. S. Lewis, "can have only an entertainment value."[11]

God's creative acts in the first chapter of Genesis bring form to the formless, establish order out of chaos, and calm the waters' power. God's creativity is unleashed so that life can flourish and civilization develop—and he invites humans (you and me) to be his partners in doing this.

"Our human creativity," writes David Atkinson, "should seek to mirror God's, . . . to confront the formless and disordered places of our world, and of our lives, and make them places of beauty and goodness."[12] Our creative acts should leave behind that which is "pleasant to the sight and good" (Genesis 2:9, ESV).

God has placed us in this world and commissioned us to unpack and unfurl all the latent potential that he has folded into creation. We're not to consume the world but to cultivate and care for it.

Everyday leaders must not fear creativity and innovation but embrace them as partners to help people and ministries flourish and reach their full potential in Christ. This is what it means to be an image bearer. This is what it means to care for and cultivate God's creation (Genesis 2:15).

Marrying Imagination and Innovation

My friend Randy Raysbrook and I left the meeting asking the same question: "How can we do this?" Our Navigators leadership tasked us to design a training process that would equip local neighborhood groups to band together to love their neighbors and live on mission. They would be called "mission outpost teams" (MOT).

A MOT is a small group located at a distance—an "outpost"—from a local church. The distance is not only physical (in miles) but spiritual (people distanced from God). Our goal was to provide the training and resources for these small bands of believers to succeed in their mission.

Randy and I asked God to give us an idea. We imagined a format different from a traditional workshop or a day-long seminar. The function was training, and this training needed a form, a way of packaging the principles. After much brainstorming and reflection, we settled on an approach never used before in The Navigators.

We created a board game!

Our model was a cross between two established games: the Ungame and Monopoly. We chose the Ungame because it didn't have winners or losers. Monopoly gave us inspiration for the game layout and the use of game cards.

A board-game format created an interactive learning experience—something groups needed to function as a team. The MOT game brought people together to explore how to think like missionaries, how to understand their neighborhood's cultures, and how to creatively start faith conversations.

We employed a graphic designer to create an attractive foldable game board, a printer who ingeniously developed a way to cheaply print this board, and found pizza boxes to package and mail the game to our staff. Hundreds of people across the US learned how to live on mission by playing a game.

Our Spirit-led imaginations created an innovative product to advance the gospel. We married *fun* to *form* (a board game) to achieve a *function* (training people). Without imagination we never would have created this ministry resource. Imagination fuels innovation.

I believe that imagination is a lost tool in ministry and should be reemployed by everyday leaders.

"Why is it that professed Christians dutifully sit in church . . . and then go out to live like pagans?" asked author and pastor Warren Wiersbe in his book *Preaching and Teaching with Imagination*. "I have a suspicion that one factor is the *starved imagination* of congregations. . . . The truths of Scripture have never penetrated their imaginations."[13]

What is imagination? Wiersbe described it as "the image-making faculty in your mind, the picture gallery in which you are constantly painting, sculpting, designing, and sometimes erasing."[14] Author Cheryl Forbes writes that "imagination is the *imago Dei* [image of God] in us. It marks us as God's human creatures."[15] Imagination is the creative act of making images that draws our senses into experiencing God's truth.

The Puritan theologian and philosopher Jonathan Edwards believed that "[imagination] can enable the mind to grasp circumstances never actually experienced."[16] Like John Calvin, Edwards wanted to evoke *suavitas* (Latin for "sweetness" "or delight")[17] in people's souls as they heard the promise of Christ. The sweetness of grace can be experienced through imagination.

God regularly appeals to our imaginations. Look at the spectacular images he paints in passages like the first chapters of Ezekiel and Revelation. These vivid pictures grab our senses to experience him. Without imagination, walking with God would be like replacing our high-definition flat-screens with a 1950s black-and-white television.

Unfortunately, the church often lives in a black-and-white world. When was the last time you heard a message or took a course on creativity and imagination? Pastor Eugene Peterson wrote that the church needs "masters of the imagination."[18]

Imagination fuels innovation; it generates new ideas, frames the obvious in new ways, and encourages new ways of thinking outside the boundaries of our typical approaches.

Describing Innovation

How is innovation different from creativity?

The common definition of innovation is the action of creating and introducing new methods, ideas, or products. These methods or products can be easily transferred and widely used.[19]

Steve Jobs is quoted as saying, "Real artists ship."[20] Everyone has new ideas, but few have the ability to bring them to completion, producing products or resources that influence others. People can be creative yet not innovative, but innovators must always be creative.

Innovation, then, creates new, tangible, repeatable products or resources that can be picked up and used anywhere by anyone. These new forms accomplish specific functions. Like Steve Jobs, we want to marry aesthetics to function, creativity to goals.

Navigators founder, Dawson Trotman, was a master ministry innovator. When someone mentions "The Navigators," one image often comes to mind. "You're the people who memorize Scripture." Scripture memory is part of our culture, the DNA of our movement. How did it get started?

Early in his Christian life, Trotman learned the power of hiding God's Word in his heart (Psalm 119:11). Memorizing Scripture changed his life. As he ministered to sailors in the 1940s, he wanted to create a "form" to encourage Scripture memory. His imagination led him to create verse cards that fit into a packet that a sailor could slip into his pocket so he could review verses anytime of the day. To encourage memory, Trotman grouped these verses around topics. This was the birth of the Topical Memory System (TMS), the most widely used tool for memorizing Scripture today.

Trotman also created an illustration to picture the Christian life. His first experiment was a three-legged stool that evolved into a wheel. The Navigators Wheel illustration is still used today.

Imagination fuels innovation, and Trotman preceded Steve Jobs by designing ministry tools that "shipped." Trotman used his imagination to innovatively create new forms (ministry resources) that were practical, portable, pass-on-able, and designed with a touch of flair. The practicality of the TMS made Scripture memory doable for anyone, even those who claim poor memories. His ministry tools were also portable—sailors could carry memory verses in the pockets of their everyday uniforms, and anyone could sketch out the Wheel illustration on a napkin while drinking coffee with a friend. These "anyone," "everywhere" principles are pass-on-able as well. Everyday Christians can learn a system to memorize the Bible or use a simple illustration like a wheel to picture the Christian life and pass it on to a neighbor, coworker, or friend.

These new ministry forms (tools or resources) innovatively accomplished some critical functions: allowing us to immerse our lives in the Scriptures and giving us a biblical illustration of the Christian life.

Growing Innovation

Innovation and imagination are like the fledgling plants in our gardens. They need nourishment and protection to grow. There are some practical things that leaders can do to grow a spirit of creativity and innovation in their ministries. Here are five imagination enhancers to incorporate into your church or ministry to grow innovation.

Encourage Loitering

In Greek and Roman mythology, the muses were nine goddesses who encouraged the arts and sciences. Over time, the nine merged into the image of one woman, the muse, who inspires creative artists.

The verb form of *muse* means to "be absorbed in thought," with an implication that creative thoughts can occur.[21] The English word is derived from an Old French word referring to the act of "pondering or loitering."[22] I enjoy this picture of loitering. The dictionary describes *loitering* as "standing around without any obvious purpose."[23] When you combine musing with loitering, you form a picture of stopping to think so that inspiration can happen. To fuel the fires of innovation in a ministry or workplace, we must give people time to loiter—to stop and think so that inspiration can happen.

"Stillness is a most fertile breeding ground for ideas," write Eric Liu and Scott Noppe-Brandon. "Frenzy is generally not a sustainable life strategy."[24] So much of life comes down to our slowing down, our purposeful loitering.

Why is slowing down important for creative insights? Much creativity and innovation results when we combine seemingly unrelated ideas or images together. This is the definition of a metaphor; metaphors bridge two seemingly unrelated ideas that, on the surface, are not equivalent or related. When we relax, our minds are freer to make those associations because the brain is not preoccupied with solving a problem or completing a task.

"Our brains are naturally associative," write Liu and Noppe-Brandon. "Our job is to feed them material to associate and synthesize."[25] Association best happens when we slow down. When we loiter—slowing life down to think—we allow our brains time to make connections, which in turn helps us be more innovative.

How can we build time into our ministries and personal schedules to slow down and think? One company has instituted the 15 percent rule; every researcher spends 15 percent of his or her workday pursuing new ideas.[26] I regularly schedule creativity days that I set aside without appointments or ministry deadlines to give me time to think and explore new ideas, read stimulating books, talk with innovative people, or visit an art museum.

Sometimes loitering needs permission. In some settings, we must have organizational permission to stop and think. Some leaders have the ability to give themselves permission. Our sense of loyalty and unhealthy assumptions about success work against taking time to purposefully loiter; we feel we have to keep working. With the Holy Spirit's guidance, we need to learn to say yes to think time.

Dedicated thinking time fuels (starts) innovation. When we fail to slow down, we stop the creative process. We can end up living the machine life that Dorothy Sayers described: "The nature of a machine is to do the same thing over and over again so long as it keeps going."[27] "Do[ing] the same thing over and over again" reminds me of the description of Edward Bear in A. A. Milne's *Winnie-the-Pooh*:

> Here is Edward Bear, coming downstairs now, bump, bump, bump, on the back of his head, behind Christopher Robin. It is, as far as he knows, the only way of coming downstairs, but sometimes he feels that there really is another way, if only he could stop bumping for a moment and think of it.[28]

We all need to stop bumping and learn how to purposefully loiter. Leaders must learn to loiter, and they must give others permission to do the same. In his insightful book *Orbiting the Giant Hairball*, author and artist Gordon MacKenzie writes that "a management obsessed with productivity has little patience for the quiet time essential to profound creativity. . . . Workers [are] being sucked inside-out by corporate milking machines."[29] We encourage creativity and innovation by making loitering a value in our lives and ministries.

Know Your Context (or End User)

How do you introduce change or innovation into a culture? Researcher Everett Rogers has documented successful and unsuccessful attempts to bring about cultural change through government services or organizations like the Peace Corps.

One documented story is about a Peruvian government worker introducing water purification practices into a village. She was enthusiastically received by people, and her practices were immediately tried. However, when she returned some time later, people had reverted to their old ways of doing things. Why didn't they embrace the new innovation?

Rogers concluded that "the diffusion campaign . . . failed because the innovation was perceived as culturally inappropriate by the villagers."[30] Why? Understanding interpersonal networks is important if change is to be embraced. Critical to this network were the local leaders who were the influencers. In this case, the local influencers were the tribal elders. It was these leaders, Rogers writes, "who could have activated local networks to spread innovation," but they were overlooked.[31]

Our zealous government worker was more "innovation-oriented" than "client-oriented."[32] As Rogers explains, "She was unable to put herself in the role of the village housewives, and thus her attempts at persuasion failed to reach her clients because the message did not suit their needs."[33] She had failed to understand her context.

Without an understanding of context, innovation is simply a novel idea. For innovation to take root, we must become culture detectives who understand the context where the innovative product, resource, or strategy will be introduced. Understanding context propels innovation.

Dawson Trotman introduced an innovative approach to Scripture memory because he took into consideration the pocket size of a sailor's uniform. He understood the end user's context and designed accordingly. Jobs understood the intuitive nature of human character and created metaphors for people to easily access a personal computer.

What stops innovation? Innovation is thwarted if we fail to

understand the context or culture of the people who will be using our resources or strategies.

Recruit the Right People

Innovation is the ultimate team sport. "Collaboration drives creativity" writes Keith Sawyer, "because innovation always emerges from a series of sparks—never a single flash of insight."[34]

Too often churches and ministries point to one or two people and say, "They're the creative ones we rely on." This does a disservice to innovation. The comment places creativity in the hands of a few, an unfair responsibility, and communicates that creative thinking is a specialized gift rather than something everyone can participate in. When we think teams, we create settings that remove innovation from an isolated few and expand it to the many.

How do you develop effective innovation teams that create a "series of sparks"? Sawyer identifies four conditions that enable innovative teams to be effective:[35]

1. Skills match the task.
2. The goal is clear.
3. There is constant and immediate feedback.
4. There is freedom to concentrate on the task.

In our earlier discussion of collaborative leadership, I emphasized that collaborative teams must have a diversity of people with different giftings, experiences, personalities, backgrounds, and expertise. Not only should different people be represented, but Sawyer notes that "their skills [must] match the challenge of the task. If the challenge is too great for their skills, they become frustrated; but if the task isn't challenging enough, they simply grow bored."[36]

Having a clear creative goal is absolutely essential for this team to function well. In the study of leaders from thirty companies that Sawyer referred to in his book (which I noted in chapter 4), unclear objectives are the "biggest barrier to effective team performance."[37]

Creating a feedback loop inside and outside refines and shapes the final innovative product. A practical approach for feedback is creating rapid prototypes. When Randy and I developed the board game for our mission outpost teams (MOT), we designed a rapid prototype on a laminated sheet of paper, introduced the game at a conference, and solicited feedback.

We asked two simple questions for quality feedback:

1. What went well?
2. What can be improved?

A feedback loop works out the bugs and quirks of innovation, and rapid prototypes enable designers to move projects along faster.

My friend Josh is the director of a music production program at a midwestern university. He's one of the most creative people I know. When asked how to encourage innovation in organizations, he replied, "Identify the lynchpins, the people who have the ability to both generate and execute ideas. The most successful projects involve many people." Innovation is a team sport.

Finally, the team must be free to concentrate on the task. Concentration happens when time is set aside for healthy interaction about the project. Research has shown that conversations are one of the most critical factors in creating an innovative flow.[38]

Innovation starts in a church or ministry when the right people are on the team. It stops when the wrong people are selected. This is not a time to prioritize status, success, or longevity. You want diversity and passion from team members to think in new ways. Church status and longevity are not requirements.

Creative teams bring people together to break new ground. Sometimes innovation happens with solitary inspiration, but most of the time it's a series of sparks from many people that leads to breakthrough strategies.

Be a Cheerleader

Quoting author Finley Eversole in her book *Walking on Water*, Madeleine L'Engle describes how most creatives are "destroyed not through the use of outside force but through criticism, innuendo," and, in L'Engle's words, "the dirty devices of this world."[39] How does this show up?

L'Engle cites some illuminating research that Eversole discovered:

> In our society, at the age of five, 90 percent of the population measures "high creativity." By the age of seven, the figure has dropped to 10 percent. And the percentage of adults with high creativity is only [2] percent![40]

When criticism and innuendo destroy innovation, we're diminished as people and our creative impulses vanish. What counters criticism? Everett Rogers writes that innovation is often adopted because we "depend mainly upon a subjective evaluation . . . that is conveyed to [us] from others like [ourselves] who have already adopted the innovation."[41] In other words, when our peers cheer on innovation, it's more likely to be embraced.

Cheerleaders in a ministry or church raise the level of creativity and innovation through empowerment and experimentation. Empowerment gives people both responsibility and authority—something I lacked in a former setting.

I was once part of a team tasked to design a series of leadership development seminars. We crafted a good plan, but when I arrived at the inaugural session, I discovered that little of it was implemented. The leadership above us changed our plan. Our team had responsibility for developing the seminars but no real authority to put our plan into action.

My task of creating a training process for our MOT was totally different. The leaders gave our team both responsibility and authority. They didn't micromanage our progress or hover over our plans. I kept them informed at regular intervals to solicit their input and insight, but they released us to carry out our assigned task. What a refreshing experience!

Healthy independence happens because we trust people. If we task people we trust, then we can release them in their responsibilities.

Cheerleaders encourage innovation by leaving room for experimentation. The reality is that not all innovative ideas, products, or strategies will succeed. After the success of our MOT board game, I worked with a workplace ministry team to develop a similar game for workplace missionaries. We spent money and time and developed a prototype but found little interest in the tool. I now have a box of Workplace Mission Teams game boards in my basement. Cheerleaders in ministry or business are willing to cheer on risk, knowing that not everything will be a success.

This runs counter to our tendency to applaud the success of similarity and reproducibility. Too often, our goal is to perfect and mass-produce current strategies or resources. We applaud success of the known rather than cheering on the new and innovative.

We must be cheerleaders for the creatives in our midst. We do this by empowering people with authority and responsibility and giving them freedom to experiment. The quickest way to kill innovation is to create an affirmation-free zone—a space where creativity goes unnoticed, unappreciated, and uncultivated. Instead, let's build affirmation-rich zones in our churches and ministries! This will bring people together for breakthrough ideas.

Add Some Flair

"Our reliance on propositions and our desire to quantify have stripped life of imagination," writes Cheryl Forbes.[42] Quantifying life and making it predictable leaves us with little flair or creative attraction. This puts a damper on innovation. Ministry innovators add flair—a touch of beauty, whimsy, or fun—to whatever they do. Flair and creativity enhance innovation.

My chapter on being a culture detective grew from a simple four-by-six-inch booklet that was originally titled *Nick Athens Cultural Detective Kit*. We designed it with a film-noir flavor and a Humphrey Bogart–like character on the cover. Nick Athens was a play on Paul's encounter with the Athenian culture in Acts 17. The theme of Nick Athens was woven through the book's various detective assignments.

We could have created a booklet with a simple text-driven cover, but we wanted to add some fun and flair and give the topic a creative twist to attract an audience. This creative twist, this inclusion of that which is beautiful or elegant, marks our works as image bearers. Any cursory glance at nature shows the creative twists that our Creator brings to his works.

Adding some flair answers the question posed by author Jean

Fleming: "What does it look like to live a beautiful life in a fallen world?"[43] Adding color, humor, or elegance creates something beautiful in a fallen world.

This quote from Madeleine L'Engle energizes my sense of flair:

> We draw people to Christ not by loudly discrediting what they believe, by telling them how wrong they are and how right we are, but by showing them a light that is so lovely that they want with all their hearts to know the source of it.[44]

As image bearers, we want to design products and resources that show people "a light so lovely" that they are drawn to look, to try, and to practice. This requires marrying aesthetics—the beautiful—to the functional. Sho Baraka writes that "methods should be a garnish for transcendent truth."[45] We "garnish" our designs, giving them a splash in look or creative color to entice people to eat. Garnish adds flair.

How can you add some flair? Here are some simple assignments to raise your "flair quotient."

1. Look around at designs and images that entice your attention. What can you learn from them?
2. What metaphors or analogies could be employed to capture your message?
3. Add the visual—an eye-catching photo, an unusual font, or a dash of color.
4. Enlist a graphic artist to give you ideas, design a cover, or critique your presentation. Graphic artists are trained to make things visually enticing.

Four Innovation Tools

Tasks remain ideals without practical tools. Over the years I've developed and used several tools to create new ideas. Following are four innovation tools that can bring people together to break new ground.

Tool No. 1: Picture It

Metaphors and analogies create word pictures, joining two seemingly unrelated things to craft new meanings. Analogies are formed when one thing is compared with another to highlight ways they are alike. For example, the Kingdom of Heaven is like a mustard seed, a sower, or yeast (Matthew 13).

Jesus referred to himself as the Bread of Life, Living Water, and Good Shepherd (John 4:10-15; 6:35; 7:38; 10:11-18). Not only do these images (metaphors) lodge in our minds, but there's also an enigmatic nature to them that draws us to think, ponder, and meditate.

Cheryl Forbes states, "Our brains naturally think in pictures. Neurophysiologists working in the area of learning and memory have discovered that the brain has a section to handle [and store] images."[46] Our imaginations are inextricably linked to memory—we remember the images we see. These "memory images" are stored and used by the imagination to create that which is new.[47]

Analogies and metaphors create these images and provide a greater probability that they will linger in our minds.

Here's a small assignment to practice this word-picture tool: Your church is exploring innovative approaches to evangelism for their adjoining neighborhoods. How would you complete the following sentence? In this neighborhood, evangelism is like _____. Brainstorm and fill in the blank with anything that comes to mind.

The songwriter John Lennon said that he would use any word that came to mind—like *cauliflower*—until he hit on the right word for a song line.[48] Go wild and create as many analogies as you can about evangelism and then pick the best ones. How could these analogies shape your evangelism strategy?

Tool No. 2: Think of the End User

Picture the people whom the ministry or event is targeted for. Put yourself in their minds and context. Ask some end-user questions:

- Who are they?
- Where are they?
- What are their interests?
- Why would you use this approach (an activity, event, etc.)?
- What would make it more learner-friendly for them?
- How can this connect with their everyday worlds?

You want to establish a strategy to connect with the neighborhood surrounding your church. Put yourself in the shoes of people living in that neighborhood—these are the end users. Then conduct a simple research exercise. Stay home on a Sunday morning and observe how many people in your neighborhood appear to be attending church. If they aren't attending church, what are they doing? Does this say anything about how they value spirituality, faith, or God? What do you think would catch their attention to bring God into their conversation about life's priorities? How would the answers to these questions affect how you think about evangelism in your neighborhood? Innovation starts when we consider the end user.

Tool No. 3: Ask "What If . . . ?"

The what-if question explores subjects without preconceived boundaries.

- "What if money were not a problem?"
- "What if everyone—or no one—agreed with us?"
- "What if we had unlimited staff?"
- "What if our ministries doubled in size within a year?"

A profitable way to generate new ideas is to fill a sheet of paper or a whiteboard with as many what-if questions as possible. After you've explored the topic, then select the best question to spend time discussing.

Let's return to your neighborhood context and ask some what-if questions.

- What if your next-door neighbors faced a health crisis?
- What if your next-door neighbors began talking about the need for faith education for their children?
- What if your next-door neighbors began questioning the role of God in current events?
- What if you chose to walk your dog every night at the same time?
- What if you became involved in a local neighborhood association?
- What if you created a babysitting co-op for parents?

Tool No. 4: Switch Places

Switching places means choosing another point of view or vantage point from the one we're used to. This can help us look at our contexts in fresh ways. We can look through the eyes of a celebrity; an actor; a pop, rap, or rock-and-roll singer; a pastor; a child; an unbelieving coworker; a fellow employee; and any other kind of person you might think of. The person's role can be friendly or antagonistic. Sometimes an antagonist gives the best ideas.

Switch places with a neighbor who constantly posts political signs in his front yard (signs you don't agree with!). Why are politics so important to him? Do you think God plays a role in his political mindscape? Why or why not? What would happen if you and your neighbor had a respectful conversation about your different points of view?

Switch places with the local workaholic—the person who consistently leaves the house at 7:00 a.m. and returns after 7:00 p.m. What drives her work habits? How is she defining *success*? What could challenge her to bring God into her priorities?

When we switch places with people, we begin to see the world from their points of view. This gives us insight into their feelings, beliefs, and values. What does switching places remind us of? It's reminiscent of the incarnation—God becoming man "and [moving] into the neighborhood" (John 1:14, MSG).

These four innovation tools are used to accomplish a task. We select the proper tool for the task at hand. Not every tool in the toolbox is meant to be used at the same time.

When faced with designing innovative solutions, choose one or two of these tools to generate new ideas. Like our earlier illustration of a funnel, you will amass a lot of possibilities that need to be funneled down to a few. What do you do next? Sleep on it.

Give yourself time to reflect and ponder the best course of action after taking a pause. It's at this juncture that the introverts on your team will shine. They will go back and not only reflect on the work so far but will probably generate new ideas. After you've slept on your idea-generating session, you can ask the Lord for wisdom in selecting and implementing the best ideas.

Everyday leaders don't have to be the most innovative people in the room. What they can do is to find innovative people and lead them collaboratively to meet ministry challenges in new and fresh ways. We can all learn to use the basic tools of innovation to create new approaches and strategies to meet ministry challenges—and we don't have to do it alone. Collaborative leadership brings people together to break new ground.

A Final Reflection: Challenges Are Opportunities for Innovation

Our Lord delights in doing new things. Unfortunately, churches and ministries often resist that which is new. It's easy to become married to our ministry forms because they're familiar and over time achieve an almost inspired status. There's something comfortable about repeating what we've always done.

Wisdom is needed to know when a ministry form—a method, tool, strategy—no longer accomplishes the function for which it was designed. For example, what happens if you can't worship together but are forced to worship online?

The Great COVID Shutdown of 2020 forced most churches to cancel in-person services for months. Pastors scrambled to plan online services. Some did the minimum, hoping that in-person worship would come back soon. Others experimented with new forms, and their ministries prospered. They saw the Great COVID Shutdown as an opportunity and not an obstacle; they prayed for wisdom to do the most good and the right thing for their congregations.

My friend Pastor Rich turned his online service into a relationally rich time. "One of our values has always been relationships," he told me. "Our leadership decided that we would not sacrifice the relational element of our ministry for a sterile stand-behind-the-pulpit, talking-head video broadcast."

How did they attack this problem with imagination? They researched a variety of online services and discovered a way to greet people as they came online for their service. "We took the normal greeters in our services and made them online greeters," said Rich. "We created a virtual lobby and provided opportunities for people to gather in groups online in the forum just as they would in a typical in-person service."

With a little imagination and effort, they innovatively turned a liability into an opportunity. When we become innovative, we trust God for new approaches—new forms—to meet current challenges. We exercise our sanctified imaginations.

The twentieth-century pastor and author A. W. Tozer painted a vision for employing a sanctified imagination:

> I long to see the imagination released from its prison
> and given its proper place among the sons of the new
> creation. . . . The stodgy pedestrian mind does no credit
> to Christianity.[49]

May the Lord bring a sense of renewal to our lives and ministries through the sanctified use of our imaginations. I pray that God would release scores of ministry innovators—everyday leaders—who are willing to take risks, boldly imagine, and bring a touch of beauty to ministry.

A Case Study in Innovation

Three things stand out about Kevin and Kent. They're twin brothers, they're doctors, and they share a passion to live on mission through their vocations. Kevin and Kent are everyday leaders, not ministry professionals. They take initiative, display Jesus, and have a direction. They're everyday physicians, not the ultra-specialists that inhabit our hospitals.

How can you get started on the way of innovation? Read the training exercise on innovation in the appendix. Identify a current challenge or need for change. Bring a small group of people together to break new ground by using this training exercise to create local, innovative strategies.

Like many physicians, Kevin and Kent have participated in short-term mission trips, using their medical skills in impoverished countries. Away from the inflexible rules and recordkeeping of standardized medicine, they could genuinely treat people and freely share their faith. Each time they returned from a trip, they were motivated to bring Christ into their medical practices.

"How can we continue this enthusiasm in our local settings," they asked themselves. "If we freely give to the medically needy overseas, how can we do the same with people in our own community?"

As they prayed and talked, a solution emerged: They imagined creating a free medical clinic. These everyday leaders began with a vision and a blank sheet of paper.

What was their first step? They gathered a group of friends to pray and plan for a medical clinic. They included me in the mix because they wanted to train people in some simple evangelism skills and prayer ministry. For months we met in Kevin's home dreaming and planning for this free clinic. We needed innovative approaches to make our local dream a reality.

We decided that the clinic's location should be outside a church building. We would make Jesus central, but the location would be in a neutral and inviting setting for the community.

The Lord opened up the local community center as our location, but there were some limitations. We couldn't set up a permanent clinic, since the building was used during the day. We would need to set up and take down the clinic each week. Fundamental needs like creating private patient rooms became a challenge. We also needed portable examination tables; we couldn't have patients sitting on folding chairs. Another concern was providing selected prescription drugs. Since our clients were people with no health insurance, how could we provide limited prescriptions and outpatient services at minimal to no cost? Finally, how could we train people to sensitively pray with patients and engage in faith conversations? These were big concerns that needed innovative approaches.

Our little team went to work. A pharmacist volunteered to research and track down prescription-drug services that catered to clinics like ours. Someone suggested using portable massage tables as examination tables. The creation of patient rooms was the most innovative.

One of our volunteers came up with a solution to the private patient rooms. He built a portable frame from PVC pipes from which you could hang curtains creating the privacy needed for a patient examination room. These frames were anchored by being screwed into empty propane tanks. You had to see it to believe it! One person's imagination created a series of portable examination rooms.

How did we secure limited hospital services like X-rays or MRIs for people with no insurance? We approached the local hospital and bartered for these services because we believed that, in time, we would save the hospital money by treating people who would typically show up in the ER units.

How could we bring Jesus into this setting without cornering people with the gospel? We trained the receptionists, nurses, and physicians to sensitively ask patients this simple question: "Would you like to pray with someone before you leave?" If they said no, our staff wouldn't ask the question again. If they said yes, they would be directed to one of our prayer partners.

This free clinic is now more than a decade old. Thousands of patients have been treated free of charge. Many have embraced Jesus. Hundreds have been prayed for. From this small clinic, four additional clinics in the state have been launched. God has been at work!

This was a model of ministry innovation. Everyday leaders took time to think, spending months praying and planning. We worked to understand our end users, brainstorming how we could create a comfortable setting for people ashamed and beaten down from a lack of medical services. We made the entire effort a team sport and had nearly one hundred and fifty volunteers each month giving time to make the clinic a reality. We used God's gift of imagination to create a weekly freestanding clinic with some flair, including empty-propane-tank curtain frames!

This medical ministry began with two everyday leaders—Kevin and Kent—and a blank piece of paper. They recruited a team of everyday leaders to create something that didn't exist. They identified a local challenge, created a local solution, and developed local innovative approaches and strategies. The clinic showed people the compassion of God, the healing touch of the gospel, and the power of people working together to break new ground. Collaboration and innovation led to worship!

The Choices We All Face

Everyday leaders make choices to be wise.

All growth implies and requires change. And change suggests risk,
a move into unknown territory, a step into the dark.

LUCI SHAW, *BREATH FOR THE BONES*

A MINISTRY LEADER FOUND HIMSELF in a compromising
situation, a result of making some bad financial decisions. These
choices came back to haunt him. His failure was exposed, he sin-
cerely repented of his actions, and he promptly resigned from his
leadership position. Gene, his associate, was now in charge.

All of a sudden Gene was faced with a myriad of decisions: how
to communicate the moral failure to the ministry, how to exercise
discipline with a restorative spirit, how to replace the disgraced
leader.

What was the need of the hour?

Gene needed wisdom. He had never walked this path before.
While the situation was similar to those of other fallen leaders, the
local circumstances made it unique to this setting. What was the

good and right thing for him to do? How could Gene nourish the fallen leader while holding him to God's just standards? What was the fair thing to do in terms of a compensation package?

Life is full of choices to seek one thing over another. Author Annie Dillard writes that "we live in all we seek."[1] Our lives are shaped by the decisions we make. Everyday leaders must make some choices to grow in wisdom. In a world without fixed answers or sure solutions, we must choose to follow the way of wisdom, a path with several forks in the road that require decision-making.

If you're like me, you naturally want God's wisdom. Like Gene, we want to make choices that are good and right. However, the development of wisdom doesn't happen automatically. We must make some hard choices to walk the way of wisdom. Let's examine four choices we must make to acquire God's wisdom.

I Choose the CHASE over Passivity

It's morning and my dog Ginger is poised for action. When we let her outside in the early morning light, she first pauses on the back step. As a coonhound, she's smelling and observing the yard. When she catches a glimpse of movement in the backyard, the chase is on! Ginger bolts from a crouching position into a sprint. She's spotted a squirrel.

Ginger loves chasing squirrels. She's bred to hunt tree animals, and squirrels are natural targets to chase up a tree. The downside to this chase is that she never captures one; the squirrels are just too fast for her. In fact, they taunt her, chattering away on their safe tree perches while watching Ginger circle the tree barking.

Wisdom is something we chase after. Consider these action-filled passages:

> Yes, if you call out for insight
>   and raise your voice for understanding,
> if you seek it like silver
>   and search for it as for hidden treasures,
> then you will understand the fear of the LORD.
> PROVERBS 2:3-5, ESV

Wisdom is gained by those who chase it. The source of wisdom should not surprise us; wisdom is what God is in his essence (Job 12:13; Isaiah 40:28). When we chase God, we grow in wisdom.

"Wisdom was an important commodity in the ancient Near East," observed Warren Wiersbe. "Every ruler had his council of 'wise men' whom he consulted when making important decisions."[2] Joseph and Daniel were wise men who served as counselors. They illustrate that wisdom is not the accumulation of knowledge but knowledge applied.

Yet God's wisdom is not given to just anyone. It's granted to those who value it above everything else and zealously hunt for it as if for hidden treasure. This seeking and searching imply that we're not naturally wise in ourselves. Wisdom must come from another source, and this source is God. He invites us to chase wisdom; he invites us to fear him.

My chase for wisdom requires effort. Author Derek Kidner notes that "where the bulk of the Old Testament calls us simply to obey and to believe, this part of it [the Wisdom Books] summons us to think hard as well as humbly; to keep our eyes open, to use our conscience and our common sense, and not to shirk the most disturbing questions."[3] Chasing after wisdom involves the hard work of paying attention, asking questions, and thinking deeply.

My chase for wisdom demands me to think. From Proverbs to Ecclesiastes, we notice that wisdom is what theologian David Atkinson calls a path of 'inquisitiveness, exploration and discovery.' This exploration challenges us to move from seeking one-size-fits-all answers to thoughtfully discovering wisdom.[4] In fact, there's an enigmatic nature to the proverbs that forces us to think and reflect. Daniel Estes notes that "Proverbs tends to be deliberately enigmatic—a strategy designed to tease the hearer to reflection." Quoting C. Hassell Bullock, Estes notes that this enigmatic approach "lift[s] the commonplace to a new level of mental consciousness."[5] Chasing after and discovering wisdom demands thoughtful effort and careful observation.

My chase for wisdom yields discernment, what author Mary Margaret Funk describes as "the art of learning how to make right choices that are appropriate for myself at a particular time, place, and stage of my life."[6] Wise people possess the "know-how" required for specific situations, they're able to "circulate and renew that knowledge by working with others," and they use discernment to solve problems or achieve goals.[7] Instead of chasing after simple formulas, wise people make the effort to grow in discernment. Wisdom is the continuous mastering of a skill necessary to do what is good and right.

Chasing and capturing God's wisdom are goals for everyday leaders. We "catch" wisdom when we make the effort, take time to think, and experience the fruit of discernment. Are you ready to move from your passivity and start the chase for God's wisdom?

I Choose FEAR over Self-Confidence

"I choose fear" violates the appeal of any self-help book. You never start with the negative! Why choose fear? I choose fear because the Bible chooses fear. I know this is simplistic, so let me explain. The fear we choose is a different kind of fear than most of us are accustomed to.

A cursory reading of Proverbs reveals that fear and wisdom are married:

The fear of the LORD is the beginning of [wisdom] (1:7).

[Mockers and fools do] not choose the fear of the LORD (1:29, ESV).

Fear the LORD, and turn away from evil (3:7, ESV).

The fear of the LORD is the beginning of wisdom, and the knowledge of the Holy One is insight (9:10, ESV).

Let's untangle the meaning of fear. Author Jerry Bridges observed that "the Bible uses the term 'fear of God' in two distinct ways: that of anxious dread, and that of veneration, reverence, and awe."[8] When Jesus repeatedly admonished people "Don't be afraid" (see Mark 5:36; Luke 5:10), he was addressing the fear of dread—a feeling of terror or an anticipation of danger. The writer of Proverbs used fear in the sense of veneration or reverence.

"[Our] reverence for [fear of] Yahweh produces wise behavior," writes Daniel Estes, and "all of wisdom is grounded ultimately in one's relationship with Yahweh."[9] New Testament scholar C. F. D. Moule noted that our ability to address God as "Father," or "Abba," in the Lord's Prayer (Matthew 6:9) "conveys not a casual sort of familiarity but the deepest, most trustful reverence."[10] Fear and relationship go together.

I picture fearing God as analogous to standing on the edge of the Grand Canyon. If you've ever visited this national treasure, or another awe-inspiring natural wonder, you're drawn in by its beauty and majesty. You want to get as close to the edge as possible to take in all the grandeur; you lean forward to embrace the spectacle. But as you lean forward to take it all in, you happen to look down. Panic! You draw back out of respect for the jaw-dropping descent. You now have a new reverence for this picture of beauty. You suddenly seem very small and vulnerable compared with the canyon's depth.

The fear of the Lord is like this. His beauty, overwhelming love, and perfect holiness draw us to him. We can't get enough of him. But when we realize the magnitude of who he is, we draw back out of respect and awe. We stand small in his presence. We're overwhelmed by his majesty.

In fearing or reverencing the Lord, I renounce my know-it-all attitude and admit that I need help. Fearing God shrivels my self-confidence, forcing me to stand small in his presence. This "fear" pulls me to him in a relationship where I seek his wisdom and guidance for my life. I long for him to instruct me in the way I should go (Psalm 32:8). If this fear were an anticipation of danger, I wouldn't come to God for help; I would hide instead. Godly fear doesn't repel; it attracts and seeks relationship with reverence.

Without the Lord's wisdom, I quickly find myself feeling lost in the tangled, rapid changes of today's culture. Feeling lost can be a good thing. Author Barbara Brown Taylor shares that "the Bible is a great help to me . . . , since it reminds me that God does some of [his] best work with people who are truly, seriously lost."[11]

The founder of The Navigators, Dawson Trotman, was lost. Before pioneering a ministry among sailors, Trotman began his ministry among teenagers. Trotman found himself struggling; the boys weren't responding to his teaching. In desperation he prayed, "Lord, You made little boys. Give me an idea." He concluded that "if God wanted it done, there must be a way to do it."[12]

Dawson understood the relationship between fear and wisdom. He was lost and needed help. It was only natural that he seek out the one who "made little boys" and ask for wisdom. This is living in the fear of the Lord, a fear that attracts me to him rather than repelling me from his presence.

Being lost is a good condition. I'm left alone with the one who is smarter than I am, who loves me, and who wants to help me. I can now properly fear and reverence him. I can now begin to receive his wisdom, praying, "Lord, give me an idea." Our loving Father doesn't want us to remain lost; he wants us to grow in wisdom.

It's decision time. Are you willing to stand small before God, admit your know-it-all attitude, confess how lost you are, and ask him—the one who knows more than you—for help?

I Choose CHARACTER over Competence

The obligatory introductions were taking place at the meeting. Everyone went around the table introducing themselves. Since this was a high-powered group of leaders, initials were linked with names. Academic titles like PhD, DTh, or MD floated in the air.

When it came one leader's turn to introduce himself, he added

RHS at the end of his name. *RHS. What does that mean?* thought one attendee to himself. At the break, he asked the owner of the RHS initials to explain what they meant. With a slight smile, the man replied, "Roosevelt High School."

We too easily equate wisdom with information, knowledge, or professional accreditation. Degrees give people a public image of wisdom. We can sometimes see this fascination with image in the makeup of church or ministry boards. The addition of a doctor, lawyer, or successful businessperson is an unspoken mark of credibility. A credentialed name provides legitimacy to the board and gives the possessor an aura of wisdom.

Now, don't get me wrong; credentialed people can be wise leaders. And full disclosure, I have some university initials after my name. However, speaking as one who has lived in an academic environment, I know that degrees don't necessarily equate with wisdom.

Character trumps competency in the Kingdom. In 1 Timothy and Titus, the apostle Paul listed forty-four qualities that should characterize church leaders. Some of the qualities overlap, but one truth is clear. Of the forty-four qualities listed, only two relate to competency: Leaders should be able to *teach* (1 Timothy 3:2; 5:17; Titus 1:9) and *manage* the church and their families (1 Timothy 3:3-5; Titus 1:7). Character trumps competency in church leadership.

The apostle James connected wisdom with character when he asked future teachers and leaders this question: "Who is wise and understanding among you? Let them show it by their good life, by deeds done in the humility that comes from wisdom" (James 3:13).

The wise man or woman is the one who lives close to God and sees more clearly into things than others do, knowing how to manage life's varied circumstances.[13] This person is also "under-standing," a well-informed person who has "a veritable mass of stored-up, useful, helpful knowledge."[14] The wise person is both insightful and well informed . . . but there's something more.

James exhorted the wise person to "show it by their good life, by deeds done in the humility that comes from wisdom" (James 3:13). The Greek word translated "good" here can mean "lovely," and James speaks of "the loveliness of goodness, the attractiveness of the good life."[15] This good life shows off by doing good.

This showing off is planted in the soil of humility. The term for humility here connotes not simply a placid, ambivalent attitude; it stems from the notion of a horse being broken of its wild nature, with its strength harnessed through a bridle. Humility is "strength under control."[16]

Humble people choose to stand small in God's presence with their self-confidence, inflated egos, or accumulated information shrunk before an all-wise God. Humility is a healthy fear of the Lord, the place where wisdom begins.

Humble everyday leaders don't use wisdom to overpower people through a position, to win a debate at another's expense, or to arrogantly assume that it's "my way or the highway!" The humility of wisdom is open and transparent in its process, seeking to woo agreement rather than force obedience through an arrogant expertise. Character surrounds the application of wisdom; it governs how we choose the good and the right.

In fact, James argued that if wisdom is not displayed in a godly way, jealousy and ambition will rule, resulting in "disorder and every vile practice" (James 3:14-16, ESV). When wisdom is rightly applied, relationships will be marked by peace, gentleness, impartiality, and sincerity (verse 17). Character marks the application of wisdom and is the soil in which wisdom grows. Character trumps competency every time.

Leadership training today is a multibillion-dollar industry. Inside and outside the church, we train people in a collection of professional leadership skills—how to form and cast a vision, how to effectively delegate, or how to create and lead teams. These skills are all good, but they place a value on competency, not character. Sadly, it seems that yearly our churches and ministries lament the fall of a leader—a highly competent author, speaker, or pastor. We too quickly promote and position people for influence by their skills and not their character. We must choose character over competency.

It's decision time. Are you willing to lay aside your trust in credentials or information and allow character to trump competency?

I Choose LEISURE over Speed

Who wouldn't want to choose leisure? Our lives are so frantic that we long for those idle moments to step off life's treadmill. Leisure is a break from activity to rest or recharge our lives.

Do you see a pattern emerging in this book? Whether we're talking about loitering or leisure, the principle and practice is similar: Everyday leaders need time to think and reflect. Introverts need solitary time, and extroverts need groups to verbally process with. No matter your personality type, you need to slow down to think.

Sometimes we plan snatches of leisure to read a book, pursue a hobby, or enjoy the company of friends. Unfortunately, our definition of *leisure* is skewed. Leisure originally meant something else, and this "something else" is what we must choose.

The Greeks and Romans considered leisure as "a time being free from the obligations of work that could be dedicated to the pursuit of knowledge and wisdom."[17] Our word for "school" derives from *skolē*, the Greek word often translated "leisure."[18] These ancient cultures exalted the importance of thinking and the pursuit of wisdom (though they used slave labor to grant this pursuit to the privileged).

Our understanding of leisure is enriched by non-Western thinking. "The Chinese character for leisure is made up of 'space' and 'sunshine.' It denotes the pause, the attitude of relaxation that creates a gap in life so the sun can shine through. In contrast, the Chinese ideogram 'busy' is made up of two characters, 'heart' and 'killing.'"[19] What a contrast in symbolism! What a way to picture leisure!

I resonate with Susan Phillips when she calls our busy lives "a circus life." We're like circus performers madly entertaining others in three frantic rings of activities. Our lives are defined by "what [we've] done lately and, perhaps, posted. This rapid movement from one spectacle [or circus ring] to another allows no time to reflect or explore."[20]

My three-ring-circus life is found in my regular checklists. I create monthly, weekly, and daily checklists so I don't forget things. I fall into the trap that Joan Chittister writes about: "We are so busy making things happen that we have little time left to think about the value of what is happening. We urgently need people who concentrate on the meaning of life rather than simply the speed, the mechanization, the computerization of it."[21] I need more leisure time, but this poses another challenge: When I do set aside leisure time, I find that my brain has been rewired. Author Tish Warren describes how "we now know that the internet is changing our neural pathways—the ubiquity of words online is actually rewiring our brains to take in small snatches of information quickly and forfeit the capacity to follow long, nuanced arguments and stories."[22]

The challenge for us today is to leave our three-ring circuses and practice true leisure. "In biblical terms," writes L. Paul Jensen, "a life crammed with activity can crowd [out] the Spirit's activity, leaving the soul empty."[23] Leisure time is soul-filling time; it allows us to stop, "be still," and hear the voice of God (Psalm 46:10).

Being still means responding to the scriptural admonition to reflect, ponder, think, and meditate. Unlike the practice of our Greek and Roman predecessors, the leisure to pursue God's wisdom is not for a privileged few but for all who embrace God's way of wisdom. The Bible instructs all of us to reflect and meditate. Consider this small sample of verses:

> Blessed is the one . . . whose delight is in the law of the LORD,
>   and who meditates on his law day and night.
>   (Psalm 1:1-2)

> I think of [the Lord] through the watches of the night.
> (Psalm 63:6)

> [All people] tell what God has brought about
>   and ponder what he has done.
>   (Psalm 64:9, ESV)

> Think over what I say, for the Lord will give you
> understanding in everything. (2 Timothy 2:7, ESV)

Poet Luci Shaw described reflection as "re-flecting—bending again, flexing inward in self-examination." When we "re-flect," we attempt to discover "the truth beneath the surface, to penetrate to the centre . . . of things."[24]

This center is what Zena Hitz calls an "inward space,"[25] where we slow down to think. This inward space can be time in the Scriptures reflecting on God's words, discovering "the truth beneath the surface" of the written page. Leisure also creates space to reflect on life. We collect experiences, ponder them, extract principles of wisdom, and turn these insights into stories to share. Leisure-time reflection helps us live out of life's depths rather than out of life's shallows.

Living leisurely is more than relaxing in a favorite chair; it's a lifestyle choice that carves out space for thinking. We cultivate a lifestyle that slows down to ponder and meditate, a life that extracts wisdom from the Word and from life's experiences. Leisure is necessary for the way of wisdom.

Leisure can be savored in a moment or in a long pause; it can be several hours set aside for reflection or a restful thirty minutes chewing over the day's events. The way of wisdom does not happen by accident. Jesus understood this, departing from a packed audience of needy people to spend time in leisure, retreating to lonely places to pray (for example, Mark 1:35). To counter the fastballs of change, we must choose leisure to grow in wisdom.

It's decision time. Are you willing to depart from the busyness of life to practice leisure? Are you willing to set aside regular time to think, reflect, and learn?

Assessing My Choices

Everyday leaders must make some hard decisions. How would you describe your practice in these four areas of choice—the chase (the pursuit of wisdom), fear, character, and leisure? Check the following boxes that are most descriptive of you.

☐ I frequently admit my know-it-all attitude.

☐ I regularly schedule time to reflect and think.

☐ I make it a practice to ask God for guidance in difficult situations.

☐ I don't mind being lost if it draws me back to God.

☐ I have a number of wise people in my life circle.

☐ I take time to learn wisdom—stopping, observing, reflecting, and acting.

☐ I too often look for wisdom in experts rather than in the Scriptures.

☐ Sometimes I equate wisdom with information.

☐ If I'm honest, taking time to think is low on my priority list.

☐ The Lord and life have tested me, and I've taken time to learn from those tests.

☐ I seek to grow in character and not only in accumulating more information.

☐ Most of my leadership training is on skills, and I seldom think about character.

☐ I'm sometimes guilty of a "three-ring" life.

☐ I regularly keep a learning journal.

☐ I have a healthy fear of God that leaves me with a sense of wonder.

What can you learn about your wisdom choices from the boxes you checked?

What can you learn about your wisdom choices from the boxes you didn't check?

What is a wisdom choice you want to affirm?

What is a wisdom choice that may require some reflection and application?

What is one action step you could take in applying the wisdom choices?

Epilogue

I BEGAN THIS BOOK WITH A VISION. We need a new type of leader. I will end this book with hope. After all, this is what leaders do: bring hope to situations that appear hopeless.

Life today can be brutal. Not only do we face an onslaught of tennis balls, but sometimes those balls hit us . . . and they hurt! Everyday leaders are bruised by a hostile political climate, economic uncertainty, and the steady drip of secularization. Church attendance is declining, the number of those with no interest in the faith is increasing, and the dominant voices are out-of-control social-media outlets. Where is our hope?

Daniel Estes writes, "The message of wisdom, which is rooted in the Old Testament, finds its biblical culmination in Jesus, the incarnate Son of God."[1] Jesus is our ultimate hope, and as the incarnation of wisdom, he helps us choose what is good and right. God's wisdom provides a beacon of hope in a dark world.

> My son, eat honey, for it is good,
> > and the drippings of the honeycomb are sweet to
> > > your taste.

Know that wisdom is such to your soul;
> if you find it, there will be a future,
> and your hope will not be cut off.
>> (Proverbs 24:13-14, ESV)

What is our hope? Everyday leader, have you noticed how the smallest lit match can be seen in the darkest room? Even the tiniest flicker of light finds a way to penetrate the darkness. What better light to penetrate the darkness of our world than that formed by the overflowing goodness of God? Practicing the way of wisdom brightens our world with God's goodness.

What is our hope? Everyday leader, have you noticed how fairness, justice, and equity dominate our current conversations? We bring hope to these conversations because God's standard of righteousness is at work in this world (Luke 1:51-52), and we have the hope that he is returning to finally set things right (2 Thessalonians 1:5-10). Practicing the way of wisdom brightens our world with God's justice.

For wisdom to bring hope, we need some hope strategies—leadership practices that generate wisdom.

Lifelong learning gives us the hope that life is not a meaningless accident but a classroom in which to gain God's wisdom. *Collaboration* is the hope that when we bring people together, we can wisely break new ground. *Cultural wisdom* gives us the hope that with understanding of context, we can wisely influence and shape the culture around us. *Innovation* is our hope that the wise creation of the new will change the old.

Join me, everyday leaders, in these hope strategies. Let's embrace the way of wisdom and bring hope to our local settings with God's goodness, a goodness that helps people and places flourish. Let's bring hope to our neighborhoods, workplaces, and churches by choosing the right—what is just and fair. Be a hero that inspires and brings hope to people as you live the way of wisdom. When we do this, we will bring people together to break new ground.

Acknowledgments

I want to thank my family. I dedicated this book to my wife, Peggy. Her love and confidence in me has made me a better author, leader, husband, and father. I also want to thank my sons, Jason and Ryan. As professional illustrators, they understand the creative experience. It's been fun to exchange thoughts on creativity, comparing the writing life with the illustrating life.

Thirty years ago I met and became friends with a Navigators staff member who inspired and modeled the principles in this book. His name is Randy Raysbook. Randy's zeal for learning, his boundless curiosity, and his passion for creativity have shaped my life. Thank you, Randy!

I'm also in debt to The Navigators. For nearly fifty years this organization has given me the freedom to innovate, collaborate, and create. I'm grateful for leaders like John Ed Robertson, Darryl Sanders, Don Bartel, Rusty Stephens, Dennis Blevins, Roy and Margaret Fitzwater, Al Engler, and Dane Allphin. Without your confidence in me, and in the Lord, this book would not exist.

I'm also grateful for my former regional staff team. They followed me into new ministry ventures and were often the guinea pigs for my ideas. Thank you, Justin, Nate, Patti, Vicki, John, Jack, Jim, Lou, Bob, and Dave. What a privilege to call you friends.

Before I ever considered writing a book, a young Navigators staff member wrote a one-page letter encouraging me to pursue writing. I didn't think I had much to say, but my friend Josh Antonuncio thought otherwise! Thank you, Josh, for your vision for my life. I still have your letter!

No page of acknowledgements would be complete without a nod to my publisher and editor. Thank you, David Zimmerman, NavPress publisher, for believing in the idea behind this book. You helped bring one of my faith dreams to reality. Thank you, Deborah Sáenz Gonzalez and Elizabeth Schroll, editors who made this book so much better. Their deft and gracious editing touch kept me focused and helped me make the complex simple. I'm also grateful for the entire NavPress marketing team. Their expertise helped place the book in your hands—the reader.

Last but not least, I'm grateful to my faithful Lord, who has serendipitously led in my life. I never pictured having a writing career, but in his grace, the Lord has done "far more than [I] could ever imagine or guess or request in [my] wildest dreams!" (Ephesians 3:20, MSG). I will end with the phrase Bach included on all his musical compositions: "*Soli Deo Gloria*"—glory to God alone! There is no more fitting way to finish this list of acknowledgments.

Appendix

Training Exercises

Lifelong Learning

Using the Four Learning Markers

Marker No. 1: Stop

Sit back and mentally review the day's or week's events. This might include such varied experiences as a significant conversation, a work conflict or success, a Bible study you lead, or an unfolding political event. Choose one event or conversation to think about and then write about.

Marker No. 2: Explore

Exploration means stopping and asking questions. Questions might include:

- Why is this event important to think about?
- What does this event reveal about my values or goals?
- What does this event reveal about the values and goals of another person?
- What does my response tell me about myself?
- What can I learn about God from this event?
- Does the Bible address this event by command or principle?

What are some other questions to ask yourself about this event or conversation?

Marker No. 3: Save

Saving means taking time not only to think but also to write down what you're learning. Select some of the above questions and record your answers. From the diversity of answers, identify one to two life or ministry lessons (maxims) that emerge. Consolidate each maxim into one or two sentences.

Marker No. 4: Do

Doing means putting into action the wisdom acquired from the event examined. An application is not necessarily a step to continue the rest of your life. It could be something simple enough to do in the next ten minutes, ten hours, or ten days. Think about and then write about the following prompts:

- What could happen if I applied this truth within the next twenty-four hours?
- How could my life be different if I live what I'm learning?
- Who could I share this lesson with?

Collaboration

Creating a Collaborative Game Plan

Select

We select people of character, contribution, and chemistry. What people come to mind that meet these qualifications?

Pause

We pause to make the Great Surrender, waving the white flag of surrender regarding our agendas and preferences.

- Complete the assignment on Philippians 2:19-24 on page 66.
- Discuss as a group the discoveries from Philippians 2.
- Discuss as a group the questions regarding the Great Surrender on page 67.

Focus

Focus means clearly defining or describing the challenge we're collaborating about to form a solution or strategy.

- Allow time for each team member to clearly articulate the challenge in writing in their own words.
- As a group, discuss what each person wrote.
- Discuss this question: What would happen if we failed to address this problem or challenge?
- Have each person describe the contribution they can make to this team.

Explore

Exploring means identifying the context and imagining innovative solutions.

- Play culture detective and discuss as a team the characteristics of the context or culture in which the challenge is happening. How can an understanding of the context affect our outcomes?
- Employ several of the four innovation tools described on pages 129–132 to create possible solutions.

Plan

Planning means deciding on a plan of action. We move from the big funnel of many ideas to one practical solution.

- What is the wisest solution of the many proposed—what is good and right?
- Decide on the *who* (individual responsibilities), *what* (action goals), *where* (specific context), *when* (deadlines), *why* (vision and challenge), and *how* (next action steps).

Training Exercise for
Cultural Wisdom
The Work of a Culture Detective

Character of a Culture Detective

This exercise may be done as a team or individually. If conducted as a team, it is suggested that you answer the questions ahead of time.

- How can I practice humility in understanding this culture?
- What are some ways that I can practice respect for this culture?
- How can I practice curiosity in understanding this culture?

Culture Detective's Investigative Grid

As a team, work through the various questions on the grid. After you have discussed your answers, summarize your findings in each of the four quadrants in a paragraph describing this culture. These findings represent your deductions or conclusions.

LANGUAGE	VALUES
What are some common words? *What words are unique to this context?*	*What do people love?* *What are their interests?*
STORY	PRACTICES
What is the "origin" story? *What is the personal story?*	*What is expected?* *What is rewarded?*

As you form your deductions, take time to discuss:

- Do we have any preconceived ideas about people (gender, ethnicity, race, age, etc.) that could color our conclusions?
- Do we have any strong opinions and preferences about how we should do ministry or where ministry happens?
- Who is our "honesty broker"—a cultural insider who can help assess the reliability and accuracy of our deductions?
- What biblical passages and principles should form our interpretive grid, helping us arrive at truth that is congruent with biblical insight?

Innovation

Tools for Innovation

Review the imagination enhancers and explore how you can incorporate them in your church or ministry.

This exercise can be completed as a group or individually. I highly recommend this as a team exercise. However, the following reflection questions should be answered before the group discussion. At this point, you are drawing from previous work on collaboration and cultural wisdom.

- What are some ways that you can practice loitering?
- Who or what is our context (end user)?
- Do we have the right people on our innovation team?
- What cheerleading do we need?
- How can we add some flair?

Review the findings from the *Focus* step of your collaborative effort.

- What is the problem or challenge you're addressing? State it in one sentence.

- Clearly describe the function (goal or need) you're focusing on in one sentence.
- What forms (tools or resources) are currently present?
- How are they adequate/inadequate to address the challenge?

Review the findings from the cultural wisdom exercise.

- How can your understanding of culture shape innovation?
- How would you describe the end user in this context?
- What limitations do you face in this cultural setting? What are some cultural advantages?

Review the four innovation tools. Choose at least two that seem most relevant and helpful to this challenge.

- Employ the tools one at a time in a group exercise.
- Designate someone to be the recorder or secretary of the ideas.
- Suspend judgment and welcome all ideas.
- Determine the next time to meet and assign people to evaluate the variety of ideas and choose the one or two that would best meet the challenge or problem.
- At this subsequent meeting, discuss the ideas that were chosen as options and prayerfully select the best one.
- Assess whether this is the wisest approach. How will it bring the most good? Is it right for this situation?

Plan.

- What are the next steps to bring this innovative solution into reality? Examine the who, what, why, when, where, and how.
- Plan a feedback loop. How can you discern what is working and what needs to be improved?

About the Author

BILL MOWRY is a veteran staff member with The Navigators and serves with their Church Ministries team. He is an author, teacher, and coach. Bill has an MA in education with an adult learning emphasis from The Ohio State University. He is the author of two books: *The Ways of the Alongsider: Growing Disciples Life to Life* (NavPress) and *Walk with Me: Simple Principles for Everyday Disciplemaking* (Moody). Bill and his wife, Peggy, live at Above and Beyond Acres in Columbus, Ohio, where they practice "yardening" and enjoy life with their dog, Ginger. Bill's passion is to help the body of Christ carry out the Great Commission in relational, thoughtful, and artful ways. You can find out more about Bill and his ministry by visiting his website (alongsider.com).

Notes

CHAPTER 1 | THE CHALLENGE BEFORE US

1. Tod Bolsinger, *Canoeing the Mountains: Christian Leadership in Uncharted Territory* (Downers Grove, IL: IVP Books, 2018), 14.
2. Bolsinger, *Canoeing the Mountains*, 19, 23.
3. Based on a conversation with physicist Eric Teller, summarized in Thomas L. Friedman, *Thank You for Being Late: An Optimist's Guide to Thriving in the Age of Accelerations* (New York: Farrar, Straus and Giroux, 2016), 33.
4. Christian McEwen, *World Enough & Time: On Creativity and Slowing Down* (Peterborough, NH: Bauhan, 2011), 84.
5. Carl Honoré, *In Praise of Slow: How a Worldwide Movement Is Challenging the Cult of Speed* (Toronto: Vintage Canada, 2004), 27.
6. Nicholas Carr, *The Shallows: What the Internet Is Doing to Our Brains* (New York: W. W. Norton, 2010), 86–87.
7. Nicholas Carr, "Hypermultitasking," *Rough Type* (blog), December 10, 2009, https://www.roughtype.com/?p=1314, quoted in Alan Jacobs, *The Pleasures of Reading in an Age of Distraction* (New York: Oxford University Press, 2011), 84.
8. Honoré, *In Praise of Slow*, 121.
9. Honoré, *In Praise of Slow*, 9.
10. Nassim Nicholas Taleb, *The Black Swan: The Impact of the Highly Improbable* (New York: Random House, 2007), xvii–xviii, 206.
11. Redistricting data from the 2020 US Decennial Census, US Census Bureau, cited in William H. Frey, "The Nation Is Diversifying Even Faster than Predicted, According to New Census Data," Brookings, July 1, 2020, https://www.brookings.edu/research/new-census-data-shows-the-nation-is-diversifying-even-faster-than-predicted.

12. Wendell Berry, *Bringing It to the Table: On Farming and Food* (Berkeley, CA: Counterpoint, 2009), 92.

CHAPTER 2 | WISDOM IS THE ULTIMATE WAY

1. Bruce K. Waltke, *The Book of Proverbs*, The New International Commentary on the Old Testament, vol. 1, *Chapters 1–15* (Grand Rapids: Eerdmans, 2004), 85.
2. Waltke, *Book of Proverbs*, 86.
3. David Atkinson, *The Message of Proverbs: Wisdom for Life* (Downers Grove, IL: InterVarsity, 1996), 45.
4. Daniel J. Estes, *The Message of Wisdom: Learning and Living the Way of the Lord* (London, UK: InterVarsity, 2020), 31.
5. Atkinson, *Message of Proverbs*, 30.
6. Eugene H. Peterson, *As Kingfishers Catch Fire: A Conversation on the Ways of God Formed by the Words of God* (Colorado Springs: WaterBrook, 2017), 196.
7. Estes, *Message of Wisdom*, 14.
8. Estes, *Message of Wisdom*, 9.
9. Estes, *Message of Wisdom*, 9.
10. J. I. Packer, *Knowing God* (Downers Grove, IL: InterVarsity Press, 1973), 146.
11. Packer, *Knowing God*, 128.
12. Estes, *Message of Wisdom*, 9.
13. Estes, *Message of Wisdom*, 10.
14. Daniel J. Estes, *Handbook on the Wisdom Books and Psalms* (Grand Rapids: Baker Academic, 2005), 219.
15. J. I. Packer and Carolyn Nystrom, *God's Will: Finding Guidance for Everyday Decisions* (Grand Rapids: Baker Books, 2008), 101–2.
16. Estes, *Message of Wisdom*, 41.
17. Madeleine L'Engle, *Walking on Water: Reflections on Faith and Art* (New York: Convergent Books, 2001), 142–43.
18. R. C. Lucas, *The Message of Colossians and Philemon:* The Bible Speaks Today (Downers Grove, IL: InterVarsity, 1980), 154.

CHAPTER 3 | THE WAY OF LEARNING

1. Peter B. Vaill, *Learning as a Way of Being: Strategies for Survival in a World of Permanent White Water* (San Francisco: Jossey-Bass, 1996), 4.
2. Vaill, *Learning as a Way of Being*, 20.
3. Gordon MacDonald, *Ordering Your Private World*, rev. ed. (Nashville: W Publishing Group, 2017), 92.

4. J. I. Packer and Carolyn Nystrom, *Guard Us, Guide Us: Divine Leading in Life's Decisions* (Grand Rapids: Baker Books, 2008), 125.

5. Oswald Chambers, *My Utmost for His Highest,* (Uhrichsville, OH: Barbour Publishing, 1995), s.v. "February 7: The Discipline of Dejection."

6. Elizabeth Barrett Browning, *Aurora Leigh,* 3rd ed. (London: Chapman & Hall, 1857), 304.

7. C. S. Lewis, *Letters to Malcolm, Chiefly on Prayer* (New York: HarperOne, 2017), 101.

8. Garry Friesen, with J. Robin Maxson, *Decision Making and the Will of God,* rev. ed. (Sisters, OR: Multnomah Books, 2004), 182.

9. Tish Harrison Warren, *Liturgy of the Ordinary: Sacred Practices in Everyday Life* (Downers Grove, IL: IVP Books, 2016), 21.

10. Kathleen Norris, *The Quotidian Mysteries: Laundry, Liturgy, and "Women's Work"* (New York: Paulist Press, 1998), 15.

11. Norris, *Quotidian Mysteries,* 21–22.

12. Colin Brown, ed., *New International Dictionary of New Testament Theology,* Vol. 1 (Grand Rapids, MI: Zondervan, 1980), 486.

13. Brown, *Dictionary of New Testament Theology,* 1:486.

14. Randy Raysbrook, personal correspondence.

15. Estes, *Message of Wisdom,* 16.

16. Not her real name.

17. Donald A. Schön, *The Reflective Practitioner: How Professionals Think in Action* (New York: Basic Books, 1983), 49.

18. Schön, *Reflective Practitioner,* 68.

19. Schön, *Reflective Practitioner,* 55.

20. *Cambridge Dictionary,* s.v. "experience [n.]," accessed May 15, 2023, https://dictionary.cambridge.org/us/dictionary/english/experience.

21. Robert K. Barnhart, ed., *The Barnhart Concise Dictionary of Etymology: The Origins of American English Words* (New York: HarperCollins, 1995), 262.

22. Wendell Berry, *The Art of the Commonplace: The Agrarian Essays of Wendell Berry,* ed. Norman Wirzba (Berkeley, CA: Counterpoint, 2002), 290.

23. Jeffrey K. Smith and Lisa F. Smith, "Spending Time on Art," *Empirical Studies of the Arts* 19, no. 2 (2001): 229–36, https://psycnet.apa.org/record/2002-17130-008.

24. As quoted in Alan Jacobs, *The Pleasures of Reading in an Age of Distraction* (New York: Oxford University Press, 2011), 86.

25. Henri J. M. Nouwen, *Discernment: Reading the Signs of Daily Life* (New York: HarperOne, 2015), 84.

26. Lore Ferguson Wilbert, *A Curious Faith: The Questions God Asks, We Ask, and We Wish Someone Would Ask Us* (Grand Rapids, MI: Brazos Press, 2022), 26.

27. Luci Shaw, *Life Path: Personal and Spiritual Growth through Journal Writing* (Vancouver: Regent College Publishing, 1997), 67.

28. Jan Johnson, *When the Soul Listens: Finding Rest and Direction in Contemplative Prayer* (Colorado Springs: NavPress, 2017), 45.

29. Kirsten Birkett, *Imperfect Reflections: The Art of Christian Journaling* (Fearn, Scotland: Christian Focus, 2022), 25.

30. Jan Johnson, *Savoring God's Word: Cultivating the Soul-Transforming Practice of Scripture Meditation* (Colorado Springs: NavPress, 2004), 91.

31. I wrote about my dad and his rich legacy in *Walk with Me: Simple Principles for Everyday Disciplemaking* (Chicago: Moody, 2021), 79–80.

32. Marshall McLuhan, *Understanding Media: The Extensions of Man* (New York: McGraw-Hill, 1964), chap. 1.

CHAPTER 4 | THE WAY OF COLLABORATION

1. Sally Nash, Jo Pimlott, and Paul Nash, *Skills for Collaborative Ministry* (London: SPCK, 2011), 1.

2. David D. Chrislip and Carl E. Larson, *Collaborative Leadership: How Citizens and Civic Leaders Can Make a Difference* (San Francisco: Jossey-Bass, 1994), 5.

3. Keith Sawyer, *Group Genius: The Creative Power of Collaboration,* rev. ed. (New York: Basic Books, 2017), 8.

4. Ryan T. Hartwig and Warren Bird, *Teams That Thrive: Five Disciplines of Collaborative Church Leadership* (Downers Grove, IL: IVP Books, 2015), 43.

5. Nash, *Skills for Collaborative Ministry,* 1.

6. Chip Weiant uses the term *uncommon sense* regularly in his work. This quotation is from a paper he wrote on "Uncommon Sense" submitted to the Christian Business Faculty Association's *Journal of Biblical Integration in Business* (2006).

7. Homer A. Kent Jr., Curtis Vaughan, and Arthur A. Rupprecht, *Philippians, Colossians, Philemon,* The Expositor's Bible Commentary (Grand Rapids: Zondervan, 1996), 132.

8. J. A. Motyer, *The Message of Philippians: Jesus Our Joy,* The Bible Speaks Today (Downers Grove, IL: Inter-Varsity, 1984), 140.

9. Motyer, *Message of Philippians,* 140.

10. Ruth Haley Barton, *Pursuing God's Will Together: A Discernment Practice for Leadership Groups* (Downers Grove, IL: IVP Books, 2012), 42.

11. Susan Cain, *Quiet: The Power of Introverts in a World That Can't Stop Talking* (New York: Crown, 2013), 93.

12. Hartwig and Bird, *Teams That Thrive*, 125.

13. Sawyer, *Group Genius*, 51.

14. Warren Bennis and Patricia Ward Biederman, *Organizing Genius: The Secrets of Creative Collaboration* (New York: Basic Books, 1997), 44.

15. Dallas Willard, *Hearing God: Developing a Conversational Relationship with God*, updated and expanded by Jan Johnson (Downers Grove, IL: IVP, 2012), 73.

16. Alice Waters with Bob Carrau and Cristina Mueller, *We Are What We Eat: A Slow Food Manifesto* (New York: Penguin Books, 2022), 78–79.

CHAPTER 5 | THE WAY OF CULTURAL WISDOM

1. Charles H. Kraft, "Culture, Worldview, and Contextualization," in Ralph D. Winter and Steven C. Hawthorne, eds., *Perspectives on the World Christian Movement: A Reader*, 4th ed. (Pasadena, CA: William Carey Library, 2009), 401.

2. Tina Stoltzfus Horst, *Dancing between Cultures: Culturally Intelligent Coaching for Missions and Ministry* (Goshen, IN: Life Development, 2017), 12.

3. Horst, *Dancing between Cultures*, 15–16.

4. Wendell Berry, *Bringing It to the Table: On Farming and Food* (Berkeley, CA: Counterpoint, 2009), 8.

5. Berry, *Bringing It to the Table*, 9.

6. Berry, *Bringing It to the Table*, 50, 73. Berry borrowed the phrase *fit the farming to the land* from J. Russell Smith.

7. Richard N. Longenecker, *The Book of Acts: The Expositor's Bible Commentary* (Grand Rapids, MI: Zondervan, 1995), 475.

8. Charles H. Kraft, *Communicating the Gospel God's Way* (Pasadena, CA: William Carey Library, 1980, 6–7).

9. Kraft, *Communicating the Gospel*, 10.

10. Guinness World Record News, "Sherlock Holmes Awarded Title for Most Portrayed Literary Human Character in Film & TV," GuinnessWorld Records.com, May 14, 2012, https://www.guinnessworldrecords.com/news /2012/5/sherlock-holmes-awarded-title-for-most-portrayed-literary-human -character-in-film-tv-41743.

11. Maria Konnikova, *Mastermind: How to Think Like Sherlock Holmes* (New York: Penguin, 2013), 11.

12. Horst, *Dancing between Cultures*, 212.

13. *Oxford Dictionary of English*, 3rd ed. (Oxford: Oxford University Press, 2010), s.v. "curiosity (*n.*)."

14. Casey Tygrett, *Becoming Curious: A Spiritual Practice of Asking Questions* (Downers Grove, IL: IVP Books, 2017), 22.

15. Greg McKeown, *Effortless: Make It Easier to Do What Matters Most* (New York: Currency, 2021), 80–81.
16. Attributed to Dr. Watson, in *The Baker Street Journal* 19–20 (1969): 160, quoted in Konnikova, *Mastermind*, 16.
17. McKeown, *Effortless*, 81.
18. Konnikova, *Mastermind*, 17.
19. Bill Mowry, *The Ways of the Alongsider: Growing Disciples Life to Life* (Colorado Springs: NavPress, 2016), 82–83.
20. Karen Lee-Thorp, *How to Ask Great Questions: Guide Discussion, Build Relationships, Deepen Faith* (Colorado Springs: NavPress, 2018), 7.
21. Konnikova, *Mastermind*, 158.
22. Konnikova, *Mastermind*, 22.
23. Sho Baraka, *He Saw That It Was Good: Reimagining Your Creative Life to Restore a Broken World* (Colorado Springs: WaterBrook, 2021), 5–6.
24. Baraka, *He Saw That It Was Good*, 9.

CHAPTER 6 | THE WAY OF INNOVATION
1. Walter Isaacson, *Steve Jobs* (New York: Simon & Schuster, 2011), 125.
2. Isaacson, *Steve Jobs*, 127.
3. Isaacson, *Steve Jobs*, 133.
4. Isaacson, *Steve Jobs*, 134.
5. Quoted in Wendell Berry, *Our Only World: Ten Essays* (Berkeley, CA: Counterpoint, 2015), 64.
6. Michael Frost and Alan Hirsch, *The Shaping of Things to Come: Innovation and Mission for the 21st-Century Church*, rev. ed. (Grand Rapids: Baker Books, 2013), 225–26.
7. Francis A. Schaeffer, *Art and the Bible* (Downers Grove, IL: InterVarsity Press, 1973), 61.
8. Scott Cairns, "Idiot Psalm 10," in *Idiot Psalms: New Poems* (Brewster, MA: Paraclete, 2014), 66.
9. Dorothy L. Sayers, *The Mind of the Maker*, ed. Susan Howatch (London: Mowbray, 1994), 17.
10. William Blake, *God as Architect*, 1794, portrayed as cover art in William Blake, *Ancient of Days* (Cheshire, England: Cool Publications, 2004).
11. C. S. Lewis, *Letters to Malcolm, Chiefly on Prayer* (New York: HarperOne, 2017), 2.
12. David J. Atkinson, *The Message of Genesis 1–11*, The Bible Speaks Today (Downers Grove, IL: InterVarsity, 2022), 62.
13. Warren W. Wiersbe, *Preaching and Teaching with Imagination: The Quest for Biblical Ministry* (Grand Rapids: Baker Books, 1994), 60–61 (emphasis original).

14. Wiersbe, *Preaching and Teaching*, 25.
15. Cheryl Forbes, *Imagination: Embracing a Theology of Wonder* (Portland, OR: Multnomah, 1986), 18.
16. Terrence Erdt, *Jonathan Edwards: Art and the Sense of the Heart* (Amherst, MA: University of Massachusetts Press, 1980), 63.
17. Erdt, *Jonathan Edwards*, 11.
18. Eugene H. Peterson, *Run with the Horses: The Quest for Life at Its Best*, 2nd ed. (Downers Grove, IL: IVP Books, 2009), 72.
19. *Oxford Dictionary of English*, 3rd ed. (Oxford: Oxford University Press, 2010), s.v. "innovation (*n.*)."
20. Isaacson, *Steve Jobs*, 144.
21. *Oxford Dictionary of English*, s.v. "muse (*v.*)."
22. Robert K. Barnhart, ed., *The Barnhart Concise Dictionary of Etymology: The Origins of American English Words* (New York: HarperCollins, 1995), s.v. "muse (*v.*)."
23. *Oxford Dictionary of English*, s.v. "loiter (*v.*)."
24. Eric Liu and Scott Noppe-Brandon, *Imagination First: Unlocking the Power of Possibility* (San Francisco: Jossey-Bass, 2009), 43, 45.
25. Liu and Noppe-Brandon, *Imagination First*, 78.
26. Liu and Noppe-Brandon, *Imagination First*, 29.
27. Sayers, *Mind of the Maker*, 46.
28. A. A. Milne, *Winnie-the-Pooh*, illus. Ernest H. Shepard (New York: Puffin Books, 1992), 3.
29. Gordon MacKenzie, *Orbiting the Giant Hairball: A Corporate Fool's Guide to Surviving with Grace* (New York: Viking Penguin, 1998), 64.
30. Everett M. Rogers, *Diffusion of Innovations*, 5th ed. (New York: Free Press, 2003), 4.
31. Rogers, *Diffusion of Innovations*, 5.
32. Rogers, *Diffusion of Innovations*, 5.
33. Rogers, *Diffusion of Innovations*, 5.
34. Keith Sawyer, *Group Genius: The Creative Power of Collaboration*, rev. ed. (New York: Basic Books, 2017), 8.
35. Sawyer, *Group Genius*, 48.
36. Sawyer, *Group Genius*, 48.
37. Sawyer, *Group Genius*, 51.
38. Sawyer, *Group Genius*, 49.
39. Finley Eversole, *The Politics of Creativity*, quoted in Madeleine L'Engle, *Walking on Water: Reflections on Faith and Art* (New York: Convergent Books, 2001), 63.
40. Eversole, *Politics of Creativity*, quoted in L'Engle, *Walking on Water*, 63.

41. Rogers, *Diffusion of Innovations*, 18–19.
42. Forbes, *Imagination*, 21.
43. Jean Fleming, *Pursue the Intentional Life* (Colorado Springs: NavPress, 2013), 31.
44. L'Engle, *Walking on Water*, 113.
45. Sho Baraka, *He Saw That It Was Good: Reimagining Your Creative Life to Restore a Broken World* (Colorado Springs: WaterBrook, 2021), 82.
46. Forbes, *Imagination*, 30.
47. Forbes, *Imagination*, 30.
48. Peter Jackson, dir., *The Beatles: Get Back* (Burbank, CA: Walt Disney Pictures, 2021).
49. A. W. Tozer, *Born after Midnight* (Chicago: Moody, 2015), 114.

CHAPTER 7 | THE CHOICES WE ALL FACE
1. Annie Dillard, *For the Time Being* (New York: Vintage Books, 2000), 172.
2. Warren W. Wiersbe, *The Bible Exposition Commentary: Old Testament Wisdom and Poetry; Job–Song of Solomon* (Colorado Springs: David C Cook, 2004), 388.
3. Derek Kidner, *The Wisdom of Proverbs, Job, and Ecclesiastes: An Introduction to Wisdom Literature* (Downers Grove, IL: InterVarsity, 1985), 11.
4. David Atkinson, *The Message of Proverbs*, The Bible Speaks Today (Downers Grove, IL: 1996), 39.
5. As quoted in Daniel J. Estes, *Handbook on the Wisdom Books and Psalms* (Grand Rapids, MI: 2005), 219.
6. Mary Margaret Funk, *Thoughts Matter: Discovering the Spiritual Journey* (Collegeville, MN: Liturgical Press, 2013), 21.
7. Robert Aubrey and Paul M. Cohen, *Working Wisdom: Timeless Skills and Vanguard Strategies for Learning Organizations* (San Francisco: Jossey-Bass, 1995), 13.
8. Jerry Bridges, *The Practice of Godliness* (Colorado Springs: NavPress, 1996), 9.
9. Estes, *Handbook on the Wisdom Books*, 223.
10. C. F. D. Moule, *The Holy Spirit* (London: Continuum, 2000), 29.
11. Barbara Brown Taylor, *An Altar in the World: Finding the Sacred beneath Our Feet* (London: Canterbury, 2009), 93.
12. Quoted in Betty Lee Skinner, *Daws: A Man Who Trusted God* (Colorado Springs: NavPress, 1974), 41.
13. J. A. Motyer, *The Message of James: The Tests of Faith*, The Bible Speaks Today (Downers Grove, IL: InterVarsity, 1985), 130.
14. Motyer, *Message of James*, 131.
15. Motyer, *Message of James*, 128.

16. Donald W. Burdick, "James," in Kenneth L. Barker and John R. Kohlenberger, eds., *The Expositor's Bible Commentary: New Testament*, abridged ed. (Grand Rapids: Zondervan, 1994), 1031.

17. P. M. Forni, *The Thinking Life: How to Thrive in the Age of Distraction* (New York: St. Martin's Press, 2011), 19.

18. Forni, *The Thinking Life*, 19.

19. I shared this in my book *Walk with Me: Simple Principles for Everyday Disciplemaking* (Chicago: Moody, 2021), 74. The information shared here about the Chinese character for *leisure* is originally from Christian McEwen, *World Enough & Time: On Creativity and Slowing Down* (Peterborough, NH: Bauhan, 2011), 188, and the information about the Chinese character for *busy* is originally from McEwen, *World Enough & Time*, 19–20.

20. Susan S. Phillips. *The Cultivated Life: From Ceaseless Striving to Receiving Joy* (Downers Grove, IL: InterVarsity, 2015), 26.

21. Joan Chittister, *The Gift of Years: Growing Older Gracefully* (New York: BlueBridge, 2008), 7.

22. Tish Harrison Warren, "The Writer," in Timothy Keller and John Inazu, *Uncommon Ground: Living Faithfully in a World of Difference* (Nashville: Nelson Books, 2020), 81.

23. L. Paul Jensen, *Subversive Spirituality: Transforming Mission through the Collapse of Space and Time*, Princeton Theological Monograph Series (Eugene, OR: Pickwick Publications, 2009), 64.

24. Luci Shaw, *Life Path: Personal and Spiritual Growth through Journal Writing* (Vancouver: Regent College Publishing, 1997), 67, 69.

25. Zena Hitz, *Lost in Thought: The Hidden Pleasures of an Intellectual Life* (Princeton, NJ: Princeton University Press, 2020), 36.

EPILOGUE

1. Daniel J. Estes, *The Message of Wisdom: Learning and Living the Way of the Lord* (Downers Grove, IL: InterVarsity, 2020), 207.